LETTERS ON DANCE
AND CHOREOGRAPHY

LETTERS ON DANCE AND CHOREOGRAPHY

AUGUST BOURNONVILLE

Translated and annotated by

KNUD ARNE JÜRGENSEN

DANCE BOOKS
CECIL COURT LONDON

Illustrations reproduced by kind permission of:
1 Musée-Bibliothèque de l'Opéra, Paris
2 Det Kongelige Bibliotek, Copenhagen
3 Det Kongelige Bibliotek, Copenhagen
4 Det Kongelige Bibliotek, Copenhagen
5 Bibliothèque Nationale, Paris
6 Biblioteca del Conservatorio di Musica, Naples
7 Det Kongelige Bibliotek, Copenhagen

Published in 1999 by Dance Books Ltd
15 Cecil Court, London WC2N 4EZ

www.dancebooks.co.uk

Copyright © Knud Arne Jürgensen 1999

ISBN 1 85273 073 0

A CIP catalogue record for this book is
available from the British Library

Design: Sanjoy Roy

Printed and bound in Great Britain by
H. Charlesworth & Co. Ltd, Huddersfield

CONTENTS

Introduction	*page* 1
Illustrations	15
The First Letter	23
The Second Letter	31
The Third Letter	35
The Fourth Letter	40
The Fifth Letter	48
The Sixth Letter	55
The Seventh Letter	63
The Eighth Letter	71

ILLUSTRATIONS

1 Jean-Georges Noverre — *page* 15

2 Anton August Bournonville — 15

3 Auguste Vestris — 16

4 Page from Bournonville's original manuscript for the first of his eight letters — 17

5 Front page of *L'Europe artiste* with the first of Bournonville's letters — 18

6 Front page of *Le Scintille* with the Italian version of Bournonville's letters — 19

7 Sample of the printed French edition of Bournonville's fourth letter — 20

ACKNOWLEDGEMENTS

Many persons and institutions have been most generous with their time and granted permission to include the material in this book. First of all the Royal Library of Copenhagen and its Manuscript Department, where Bournonville's diaries are now kept. It was thanks to the discovery of some notes in the 1860 volume of his diaries that I first became aware of the existence of his eight public letters, published in the Parisian weekly *L'Europe artiste* between 8 July and 26 August 1860.

Other debts to be acknowledged are, of course, the valuable suggestions and practical assistance I have received from the other libraries and collections that I have approached during the research and collecting of the material included in this book. Two French curators are of major importance here: Mme Else Dahl-Delaunay of the Département des Périodiques at the Bibliothèque Nationale in Paris, and Monsieur Pierre Vidal, *conservateur en chef* at the Musée-Bibliothèque de l'Opéra. For assisting me in the English translation of Bournonville's at times rather archaic French I am particularly grateful for the careful editing undertaken by Richard Glasstone, and for the unfailing support received from Mrs Virginia Laursen and from my friend Dr Luca Bianchedi.

Finally, I am infinitely grateful to the publisher, David Leonard, for having undertaken this project and for his continued interest in my Bournonville studies during this last decade.

KNUD ARNE JÜRGENSEN
COPENHAGEN 1999

This first English edition of August Bournonville's
LETTERS ON DANCE AND CHOREOGRAPHY
is dedicated to

ANN and IVOR GUEST

EDITORIAL NOTE

Words that were *italicised* in the original source have been retained as such in this translation. Words which Bournonville inserted, changed or omitted when he revised the published text of the letters for his own planned edition of these letters are shown in [square brackets].

INTRODUCTION

Throughout his professional life the great nineteenth-century Danish choreographer and ballet-master, August Bournonville (1805–1879) worked with the same enthusiasm and dedication at his writing desk as on the stage. He had already written a booklet about his art during his years of study in Paris in the late 1820s, which was published in Copenhagen at the end of his engagement there in 1829.[1]

The most important period of Bournonville's public writings, however, began after he had ended his performing career in 1848. In the following three decades he published an impressive series of articles, longer essays and books on aesthetic, philosophical, historical, social and other cultural subjects.[2]

Through these writings he became widely known in his time as a polemicist. While many of his essays delve deep into aesthetic and philosophical aspects of his art, others deal equally thoroughly with other aspects of life, so diverse that even today one might find it difficult to associate these wide-ranging writings with an artist of the theatre.

Bournonville's purpose in writing on these multifaceted sides of life can nevertheless be traced back to his profound

---

[1] This book is entitled *Nytaarsgave for Dandse=Yndere, eller Anskuelse af Dandsen som skjøn Kunst og behagelig Tidsfordriv* (Copenhagen, C. A. Reitzel/Fabritius de Tengnagel, 1829). It was republished in 1977 in an English translation by Inge Biller Kelly in an edition of 250 numbered copies (London, Royal Academy of Dancing, 1977).

[2] *See* Knud Arne Jürgensen, *The Bournonville Tradition: The First Fifty Years, 1829–1879, Vol. I, Appendix B: The Literary Works 1824–1879*, pp. 151–192 (London, Dance Books, 1997).

sense of a need to assert himself in the public's eye as an intellectual, not just as a man of the theatre. His writings often grew out of a century-old critical tradition in theatrical life that questioned how seriously performing arts institutions treated the art of theatrical dance and its staff.

A shining example of this is his series of eight French articles published in Paris in 1860 under the common title *Lettres sur la danse et la chorégraphie*, clearly modelled on the similar series of public letters written by the great eighteenth-century French reformer of ballet, Jean-Georges Noverre, which were published exactly one century before Bournonville's letters.

In his series of eight articles Bournonville reveals himself as a man of spirit combined with a profound sense of social justice. While discussing the artistic and aesthetic aspects of the ballet of his times in fine detail, he also devotes equal space to an analysis of the often miserable conditions under which the artists of the ballet lived in those days. His polemic here is, if anything, moral, indeed moralistic in nature, and always based on his deep Christian faith.

In spite of the great literary and historic value of these letters they have until recently remained completely unnoticed in the archives, and have consequently never been known to Bournonville scholars. This is even more remarkable when one considers the fact that these public letters represent the only substantial collection of essays that Bournonville ever wrote for an international audience of readers. Very few other literary works from his pen are written in languages other than his native Danish. His French public letters are therefore of extraordinary importance as a source for understanding Bournonville's personal views on his own art form when seen from an international perspective.

Moreover, these letters not only reveal many interesting aspects about the historical development of French ballet since the times of Noverre until the late Romantic ballet; they also provides a rare insight into some of the main problems that tormented not only Bournonville but many other true lovers of the ballet during the last century.

Bournonville's *Letters on Dance and Choreography* are the direct result of a series of conversations he held with the editor of the well-known Parisian weekly *L'Europe artiste*, Charles Desolme,[3] during a three-week visit to Paris in May 1860. In his meeting with this man of letters, Bournonville seems to have found a like-minded person who was just as seriously and honestly interested in the artistic progress of ballet as Bournonville himself. Desolme had earlier printed a long series of similar essays by the great nineteenth-century Italian choreographer and theorist of dance, Carlo Blasis.[4] Moreover, during the same months that he published Bournonville's letters, Desolme printed yet another series of newly written essays by Blasis.[5] One might, therefore, regard *L'Europe artiste* as one of the main if not the most important literary forum for ballet lovers of the

[3] Laurent-Pierre-Charles Desolme (1817–1877), French journalist and editor. After an impressive career with the leading French papers he founded the Parisian weekly *L'Europe artiste* in February 1853. It was later renamed *Journal général des théâtres, de la musique, de la littérature et des beaux-arts* and existed with this title until 1905 when it was absorbed by the weekly paper *La Plume littéraire et sociale*. It re-emerged in 1933 with the new title *L'Europe artiste: Grand journal d'informations artistiques* and continued for three more years until it finally closed in 1935. During its first years *L'Europe artiste* was published in both a weekly and a daily version that were slightly different in that they contained different series of *feuilletons*. Bournonville's 1860 series of eight articles appeared in the weekly version (a microfilm copy is now in the Département des Périodiques of the Bibliothèque Nationale, Paris).

[4] Carlo Blasis published his series of eight articles in the weekly version of *L'Europe artiste* between October 1855 and May 1856 under the common title *Dissertations & considérations esthétiques sur la danse et la chorégraphie* (a copy is now in the Musée-Bibliothèque de l'Opéra, Paris).

[5] The 1860 series of articles by Carlo Blasis were published in the daily version of *L'Europe artiste* between July and September with the common title *La Danse et les étoiles chorégraphiques* (a copy is now in the Département des Périodiques of the Bibliothèque Nationale, Paris).

time, in Paris and worldwide. This theory is further supported by the fact that Bournonville's letters became known in most of Europe almost immediately after they were published in Paris; they were, for instance, reprinted in an Italian version in the Turin weekly *Le Scintille* during the same months they appeared in Paris.

Bournonville's eight articles are written in a smooth, easily readable prose, almost as if they were a recording of his own slightly ornamental archaic voice during his conversations with his French editor.

Seen from this perspective, Bournonville's aesthetic and technical essays on his art set the framework for some of the most important issues for ballet during the entire Romantic period. With these letters, therefore, he stands among the most significant polemicists and theorists of dance in the modern age, comparable not only with his distant predecessor, Noverre, but also with his contemporary fellow choreographers, Carlo Blasis and Arthur Saint-Léon, and with leading dance theorists of the twentieth century.

In these eight public letters Bournonville appears almost to have needed the medium of writing to channel a torrent of creativity that could not be directed totally into dance. His letters are written with an infectious Kierkegaardian brio and garrulousness, and contain thoughts about his art, his colleagues, many people of consequence, the political-cultural crises of the ballet in his time, and moral advice to dancers and fellow balletmasters.

From this broad and yet highly concise mosaic of themes, Bournonville is revealed as a man of wide cultural interests with a reflective turn of mind. His nature was clearly firm but kindly, open to all aspects of life, and, as one might expect in a choreographer and mime, he had an expert eye for registering the colours and details of human behaviour and cultural values.

The huge sum of life experience that he had gathered before writing these essays thus clearly seems to have made Bournonville grow more rather than less tolerant in his mature years. His polemics are never bitter, but rather the expression of a self-serving yet humble man and artist who is torn by the social and cultural conflicts surrounding his chosen art form.

His strong personality shines through the self-assured yet humble tone, and the theatrical sense of performance that characterises so much of his writings comes alive, almost as if his audience of readers were sitting before him at his writing desk.

In the first letter Bournonville provides his readers with a general account of the artistic and historic developments of ballet in France since the time of Noverre up to the pre-Romantic era. It is interesting here that Bournonville directly addresses the editor of *L'Europe artiste*, almost excusing himself for having undertaken the task of analysing and assessing the 'internal French affairs' of ballet. It shows that although Bournonville spent nearly all of his creative life in the distant town of Copenhagen, he regarded himself as part of the French cultural world, especially in his mature years, and consequently felt a share of responsibility for how it progressed. His remarks about his two greatest ideals in French ballet, Jean-Georges Noverre and Auguste Vestris, are both fine and detailed miniature portraits that not only illuminate their personalities and individual characters but also show how much Bournonville identified with these two great men of the ballet.

Bournonville's balanced sense of how to deal with ballet history becomes particularly evident in his second letter, in which he considers his methods when studying and learning from dance history:

> There is nothing more difficult than comparing artists who have graced the stage at different times. Nothing remains but

tradition or a few ephemeral impressions; memories either fade away or assume fabulous dimensions, according to the character of those who transmit them; moreover, for young people the present is all, whereas old men dwell only in the past; serious analysis and fair judgement are hindered by the one group's disbelief and by the other's regrets and bitterness. Let us try to fall into neither of these extremes, and aiming at nothing but the interest of an art which has charmed the leisure of our fathers and which will be a part of our children's honest pleasures, let us see if, among the shadows of this magic lantern, we are able to learn a salutary lesson.

The same is true when he discusses the permanent conflict of interest that seems to exist between true connoisseurs and the general audience on how to judge the merits of a ballet artist:

As long as theatrical dance has existed, audiences have had their declared favourites, and the public and the *maîtres* have rarely agreed on the merits of first-rank artists. Whilst the professors were extolling the virtues of perfection of detail, the amateurs concerned themselves with the charm of the whole, demanding from talent nothing but the echo of their own feelings.

Bournonville's views on the theatre audiences of the eighteenth and nineteenth centuries expressed in his second letter also show that although eighteenth-century connoisseurs of ballet consisted almost exclusively of highly skilled intellectuals or professionals in other fine arts, the theatre audience in his own century consisted mainly of 'an assembly of people' whose primary interest in dance was to look for 'elaborate surprises, oddities of imagination, sloppy voluptuousness, bacchic joy, gross sensuality, delirium and insanity', which had caused the

Paris Opéra to develop into 'a sick and enfeebled man'. Consequently, Bournonville advocated that the education of the audience of his time was just as important as the progress of the art form. Since the lifeline of all the theatre arts is basically a question of reciprocal 'giving and receiving', Bournonville here seems to suggest that both artists and audience were jointly responsible for what he regarded as the 'decadence' of ballet during the mid-nineteenth century.

As a counterweight to these rather pessimistic reflections, in his third letter Bournonville speaks about some of his personal ideals in ballet and dance technique. It is interesting here to note his fine description of the artistic balance between the male and female dancers during the first two decades of the nineteenth century. Moreover, it is fascinating to learn that it was a characteristic muscular elasticity in the style of both male and female dancers that represented the 'exquisite finish' of their execution in those days, and allowed the dance technique of either sex to unite in a truly artistic whole:

> In the period between 1807 and 1830 [. . .] the reputation of the men was at least equal to that of the women; their success was naturally shared, since their energy, masculine elegance and polished schooling earned the audience's esteem for the *danseurs*; just as their flexibility, the *exquisite finish* of their execution, and their feminine grace, together with the heart's temptations, achieved, as they have always and everywhere, the triumph of the fair sex. It is certain that the above-mentioned epoch was one of real progress. This was due as much to the superior gifts of the leading figures of the day as to the abundance of secondary talents.

Of particular interest too is his concise assessment of Marie Taglioni, perhaps the greatest of all nineteenth-century ballerinas; here Bournonville clearly points out that both connoisseurs and amateurs instinctively understood the extraordinary performing qualities of this great artist:

> The arrival of *Mlle Marie Taglioni* (1827) heralded a new era for the dance at the Opéra. This excellent dancer had an expression of innocence, a youthful freshness that, without inspiring voluptuousness, charmed the heart with endless pleasure. She was a real sylph, a daughter of the waves, a virtuous maiden, a young lady of good family, in short everything that can be imagined as pure, gracious and poetic, combined with a talent whose outstanding quality was an airy lightness. It gave great satisfaction, both to the professional and to the amateur, to see her appear on stage, since the former was happy that he too professed such a charming art, and the latter was struck by a poetry he had not previously thought it possible to find in dance; finally, she represented to me the living image of *Terpsichore*, in spite of the imperfections that more malevolent eyes than mine took the trouble to try to find in her. The finest praise of her, and thus of her profession, was expressed by a serious old gentleman who, on his way to a performance by the famous dancer, told me in passing: "Sir, I am going to the Opéra to have a lesson in good taste."

The fourth letter deals mainly with the three greatest ballerinas of the Romantic ballet, Marie Taglioni, Fanny Elssler and Carlotta Grisi, and their respective artistic merits. Bournonville's expert eye here provides us with dance biographies *en miniature* that are interesting for what they tell us about the individual dance style and great musicality of these leading ballerinas.

In his fifth letter Bournonville moves into a more specific and technical field of his art, namely dance notation. After briefly discussing the general history of dance notation and its merits in preserving works from the past, he moves on to describe, in wise and fascinating words, why he recommends a shorthand dance notation as a useful tool for all choreographers and ballet-masters. On the other hand, he also openly criticises *La Sténochorégraphie*, the monumental notation system published by his fellow choreographer Arthur Saint-Léon in 1852; Bournonville found this work as impressive as it was difficult to employ for everyday use.

In the second part of Bournonville's fifth letter we are given what is probably the most witty and ironic description of the ballet of his time that he ever wrote. In analysing the genre of the *pas de deux* as practised in Paris during the mid-nineteenth century, Bournonville seems to have abandoned all restraints, speaking to the reader directly from his heart with an irresistible sense of humour, if not sarcasm.

In this letter he gives an ironic, even merciless description of what he regarded as the most reprehensible way to deploy the genre of the dance duet. Moreover, he provides a fine insight into the degree of 'degradation' to which he felt the art of *pas de deux* had fallen during the late Romantic ballet. His assessments are interesting, for he even publicly reproaches one of his best friends and fellow choreographers, Jules Perrot, for having partly given in to what Bournonville himself regarded as an impermissible 'lasciviousness' in dance.

In his sixth letter Bournonville analyses the Paris Opéra's practice of incorporating large divertissements in all major new opera productions. The presence of ballet in opera has a long history, almost as long as that of opera itself. Particularly in France, where true opera was slow to develop, the favourite musical entertainment of royalty and nobility was named *ballet de cour*, and consisted of lavish productions focusing on dance forms. This distinctive French connection between ballet and opera persisted for centuries, and reached its heyday during the middle of the nineteenth century. In contrast to the contemporary Italian tradition, in which dance always constituted a theatrical element completely separate from the opera, ballet was always considered an integral part of French opera, of grand opera in particular.

A pure product of the Paris Opéra was born in the early 1830s thanks to the industry and artistic flair of its director, the legendary Docteur Louis Véron. Only too aware of the profound social changes taking place in French society during the reign of Louis Philippe, Véron applied himself to providing the Parisian public with performances that would meet in full measure the standards and expectations of the prosperous new bourgeoisie. In order to achieve this, the noble entertainment of opera soon developed into performances of hitherto unknown magnitude and scenic splendour, such as would satisfy this clientele of newcomers to the theatrical arts.

It is interesting, in this context, to read Bournonville's remarks about the part played by theatrical dance in this process: he seems almost to believe that ballet suffered more than it gained from the new and more prolific rôle granted to theatrical dance in French grand opera. According to Bournonville, ballet was never really employed for truly artistic purposes in the French opera, but rather as a symbol of the 'exaggerated luxury of the mise en scène' that characterised the Parisian theatres during the mid-nineteenth century. It is, therefore, interesting to read his fine and very telling comparison of the *mise en scène* of French and Italian operas during the whole Romantic period:

> One can only approve the simplicity of the spectacle in operas of Italian origin. In these the singing, and sometimes even the dramatic acting, have pride of place; but one does not go to see them in order to wax ecstatic over the gifts of

the female dancers, the painters, the stage mechanics, the costumiers and so on; one does not go to see them in order to be dazzled by the rays of an electric sunrise or fascinated by the sound of a real waterfall.

Several modern authors have dreamt of a future based on the amalgamation of the combined resources of drama, opera and ballet. I believe, without any presumption, that I can foresee the fate of Babel awaiting this mixture of means. Let us have the same aims, agree mutual methods of instruction, thrust aside all narrow-minded jealousies, but let us avoid fusion, and with the arts, as with fine wines, let us not blend them.

In the same letter Bournonville also defines in brief and concise words what he regards as the ideal of a *ballet d'action* and the basic conditions necessary to make a ballet-master develop into a true artist:

We now reach the important point, central to my topic, the kind of lyric drama in which the instrumental music lends its voice to the gestures and the steps, preventing them from being a *language of dumb signs* [. . .]

The *ballet d'action* is the true school of expressive pantomime; of motivated and meaningful dance; it is where the dancer is formed into a true artist.

This genre, placed in between drama and opera, borrows from the one in order to lend to the other. Less hindered by the *unities* and free from the limits of language, it is closer to the study of nature, more accessible to people of different nationalities than all the competing arts; and wherever the movement of crowds and machinery is involved it reigns supreme. [. . .]

The *maître de ballet* must make it a point of honour to

devise the plans or libretti for his ballets himself. If he lacks the inventiveness needed to connect the various aspects of his composition dramatically, it can then no longer be said to be his own. I do not argue against the merit of a possible collaboration; but the choreographer who only composes according to a given programme is no more advanced than the musician who only orchestrates others' melodies, or the mason who rough-hews the marble for the sculptor, or the craftsman who illuminates an artist's images; he is like a hen who hatches out a duck's eggs.

The seventh and eighth letters are clearly those in which Bournonville moves with most muscular immediacy and practical sense. Born into a cosmopolitan and dignified theatrical family, he seems, since his early youth, to have been determined to elevate the intellectual and social status of his art form and its artists. It is, therefore, interesting to note that having achieved most of his goals in raising the social position of his colleagues at home, in these letters Bournonville fearlessly set out to elevate that of the dancers in what was the main temple of European ballet, the Paris Opéra. In these final letters he speaks out to his contemporaries with great ardour and indignation; but, perhaps more importantly, he also suggests many concrete proposals and practical means by which the social status of dancers could be raised.

These letters, furthermore, provide us with a true picture of the working conditions under which the artists of the Paris Opéra ballet lived in those days. In these essays Bournonville seems to have written – for an international forum – his spiritual and intellectual testament based on his life-long experience and his struggle in his home town for social justice.

How, then, were Bournonville's letters received in his own day? A few months after the eighth and final letter had been

INTRODUCTION 13

published he received, among many other letters, one from a dear and long-standing friend and colleague in Paris, the French dancer and ballet-master Edouard Carey. In a few carefully chosen words to his old Danish friend, Carey expressed how much Bournonville's essays were appreciated by himself and by many other fellow dancers in Paris:

> Dear and excellent *Maître*,
> How can I express the happiness that I have felt from reading your words? By directing your reflections towards our capital you have said: There I will still find some hearts devoted to my feelings. Your essays are written with incomparable spirit and lucidity, and on a very limited number of pages you have succeeded in unfolding more than fifty years of artistic life. I myself have pasted your articles into a small volume which I will carefully preserve as a true relic.[6]

The fact that Bournonville's letters were almost immediately reprinted outside France is another clear indication of the general appreciation given them during his own time.[7] The profound reforms suggested to his contemporaries in his two final letters are indeed so far-sighted that in retrospect one is left with the impression that these reforms, by their example alone, may have been decisive contributions to the great progress of

---

[6] Edouard Carey (1824–1873), French dancer who worked at the Paris Opéra in the mid–1830s and early 1840s. He also appeared at most of the other leading European theatres. His elder brother, Gustave Carey (1812–1881) was, at Bournonville's personal recommendation, entrusted with the artistic direction of the Royal Danish Ballet between 1861 and 1864. Edouard Carey's friendship with Bournonville lasted for many years, as witnessed by their long correspondence. The letter quoted here is dated *Paris 11 Janvier 1861* (Det Kongelige Bibliotek, Copenhagen, call no. NKS 3258, A, 4°, III, facs. 2, no. 24).
[7] The first five letters were published in Italian in the Turin weekly *Le Scintille* between 1 and 23 August 1860 (a copy is now in the Biblioteca Musicale del Conservatorio S. Pietro a Majella, Naples).

the ballet at the Paris Opéra that we have witnessed during this century.

With the rich information that Bournonville's letters provide about this focal point in the history of European ballet, it seems fully justified that his essays are now made available in a collected edition for today's dancers, audiences and for all those who treasure the traditions of ballet. In fact, Bournonville himself had considered a collected edition of these letters, as is clear from his notes pencilled on the original wrapper that still contains his autographed manuscripts. Here he states: 'contains manuscripts that can be reused on later occasions or published after my death'.[8]

With this collected and annotated edition of August Bournonville's complete *Letters on Dance and Choreography*, his wish has been fulfilled – and, I hope, in the manner that he intended and by which he wished to be remembered.

KNUD ARNE JÜRGENSEN
COPENHAGEN 1999

---

[8] Det Kongelige Bibliotek, Copenhagen (Manuscript Department, call no. NKS 3285, 4°, 7).

1 Jean-Georges Noverre (1727–1810), whose book *Lettres sur la danse et les ballets* (1760) was the model and main source of inspiration for August Bournonville's own series of eight public letters on dance and choreography, published exactly a century later.

2 Anton August Bournonville (1805–79), author of the eight *Lettres sur la danse et la chorégraphie* published in 1860.

3 Auguste Vestris (born Marie-Jean Augustin, 1760-1842), French dancer and teacher of August Bournonville, who devoted a section in his first letter to the memory of this great artist.

4 A page from August Bournonville's original manuscript for the first of his eight public letters, published in the Parisian weekly *L'Europe artiste* between 8 July and 26 August 1860.

5 Front page of the Parisian weekly *L'Europe artiste* (8 July 1860) with the first of eight articles by August Bournonville entitled *Lettres sur la danse et la chorégraphie*.

6 Front page of the Turin weekly *Le Scintille* (1 August 1860) with the Italian version of August Bournonville's *Letters on Dance and Choreography*.

QUATRIÈME LETTRE
Sur la Danse et la Chorégraphie.
(suite)

Par suite du nouveau système d'administration des théâtres subventionnés, l'Opéra cesse d'être une institution d'arts et devint tout simplement *une affaire*. Confié aux soins d'un calculateur habile, ce théâtre ne tarda pas à subir les conséquences du principe adopté par toutes les entreprises secondaires, celui de *l'isolation des artistes de premier rang*.

L'ensemble et la concurrence du talent étant jugés superflus, on y suppléa par le luxe des accessoires; l'avenir de la scène devenant une chose pour ainsi dire indifférente, il ne s'agit plus que de concentrer les effets, d'exciter la curiosité..., faire de l'argent, et, pour cela, il fallut mettre en évidence le plus possible un seul sujet marquant, une poule aux œufs d'or, sauf à changer suivant la durée ou les caprices de la vogue.

L'immense succès de Mlle Taglioni servit admirablement ce système; son nom, annoncé sur l'affiche, suffisait alors pour remplir la salle; toute rivalité fut regardée comme dangereuse, en ce sens qu'elle eût pu détourner l'attention de l'objet principal, et bientôt il ne resta autour de la célèbre artiste que des danseuses plus ou moins *figurantes* et un nombre très-restreint de danseurs. La divinité, seule et sans partage, ne tarda pas à éprouver l'inconstance de ses fanatiques; une étoile nouvelle apparut dans Fanny Essler, arrivée de Vienne, berceau du talent de cette incomparable sylphide, et entourée d'un mystère historique qui, pour une certaine classe d'amateurs, fut un attrait de plus.

Le genre de Fanny Essler était moins pur, moins parfait, sans doute, que celui de Marie Taglioni; mais il était alors conforme aux idées qui, en dépit des saines doctrines, envahirent le domaine des arts en général et de la danse plus particulièrement.

La danse de Taglioni était essentiellement *chaste*; celle d'Essler respirait *la volupté*. Un spirituel critique établit entre elles le parallèle du ciel d'azur en son vermeil. C'était vraiment la différence du nord au midi, de Jenny Lynd à la Malibran, de Thorwaldsen à Canova. La première nous transporté la danse dans les régions éthérées; l'autre la ramena dans les tièdes éléments du paradis de Mahomet. Avec Taglioni, on oubliait le théâtre et le monde; avec Essler, on courait risque d'oublier tout. Et, en effet, les créations vaporeuses de la sylphide aux ailes transparentes s'évanouirent au bruit du tambourin de la Gipsy. Le public oublieux fit comme piqué de la *tarentule*; il se laissa ensorceler par la *Chatte métamorphosée en Femme*, et perdit entièrement la tête au son des castagnettes de la *Cachucha*. Cette danse espagnole idéalisée fit époque dans les annales du ballet de l'Opéra. Intercalée dans une scène du *Diable boiteux*, elle décida du succès de l'ouvrage entier. La taille élégante, le délicieux abandon, et par-dessus tout les yeux étincelants de la belle danseuse, prêtèrent un charme énivrant à ce pas seul, qui, par sa facilité et sa brièveté même, donna lieu à des *bis* réitérés et causa un entraînement qui alla jusqu'au délire. C'était, pour ainsi dire, une lutte d'amour entre l'actrice et le spectateur, qui, se croyant seul favorisé au milieu de la foule, aurait pris en haine tout homme figurant à côté d'elle comme objet de sa coquetterie. Aussi cette jalousie toute d'imagination fut-elle parfaitement comprise par Fanny, et, pour tranquilliser les adorateurs, elle créa un emploi spécial pour sa sœur Thérèse, danseuse habile et correcte, mais que sa stature de garde du corps éloignait de la catégorie des nymphes et des bergères. Cette sœur fidèle se dévoua entièrement au service et aux succès de sa cadette; elle la soutint dans les groupes, remplit les intervalles, soutint avec résignation les froideurs du public, et poussa même la condescendance jusqu'à s'habiller en homme pour écarter de l'enchanteresse toute assistance masculine.

C'est à partir de cette époque que commença la proscription des danseurs, et les organes de la presse périodique appuyèrent cette mesure par tous les motifs que leur fournirent les ridicules ou les imperfections de certains individus qui furent désignés comme types du genre. Dès qu'on trouva parmi les *dames* un nombre suffisant de personnalités capables de renoncer aux grâces pudiques de leur sexe, les *bergers*, *majos*, *hussards* et *mousquetaires* ne furent plus représentés que sous les traits et les formes de jeunes filles, et les *messieurs*, réduits à l'état de comparses, ne figurèrent que dans les cas les plus urgents et comme un inconvénient inévitable; trop heureux encore quand ils n'étaient pas contraints de s'affubler de robes de femmes pour compléter le bouleversement de toute illusion dramatique.

Un siècle auparavant, plusieurs grands théâtres d'Italie, n'admettant pas la danse au nombre des exercices convenables à la dignité du beau sexe, avaient fait danser de jeunes garçons en femmes; c'est peut-être de là que dérive le *musqué*, le *décolleté* de certains danseurs italiens; mais, à l'époque où je m'arrête, l'extrême opposé semblait avoir prévalu. L'art de la danse n'étant regardé que comme un appel au sensualisme, et par là même descendu au rang des divertissements d'hommes sérieux et *vraisemblable*, et l'idée du *harem* exclut naturellement toute espèce de concurrence male. Aussi la faction dominante n'épargna-t-elle aucune persécution pour détruire moralement une classe estimable d'artistes qui, par le caractère de l'exécution, et même par l'enseignement et la composition, renfermait en elle les éléments indispensables d'une branche théâtrale à laquelle s'attachait ainsi la gloriole de suprématie française.

La danse des hommes fut bafouée et avilie à tel point que le contrecoup s'en ressentit hors des limites du théâtre, car les jeunes gens qui ne dédaignèrent pas de se livrer au plaisir de la danse la parodièrent par des contorsions hideuses et obscènes qui, aux yeux de l'étranger, constituent aujourd'hui la danse nationale des galants français.

De toutes les productions artistiques de Fanny Essler, aucune n'eut la popularité de *la Cachucha*, et son triomphe fut à son apogée devant le public espagnol de la Havanne.

Ce fut le signal d'une irruption générale des *Bailadores* de la Péninsule. Pour plaire aux différentes populations d'Europe, avides de sensations piquantes, ils renchérirent tellement sur le désinvolture de leurs danses, déjà parfaitement scabreuses, qu'elles finirent par devenir méconnaissables aux yeux mêmes des Espagnols, et je suis persuadé que les compatriotes des Calderon et des Murillo doivent désavouer, en rougissant, ces énormités qui, à l'égal des vins auxquels on ajoute une forte dose d'alcool, à l'usage des palais blasés, allant de plus fort en plus fort, atteignirent un degré de licence impossible à décrire, à moins de tomber dans le cynisme.

Et cependant, ces danses, soi-disant nationales, qu'on irait en vain chercher dans les lieux honnêtes, tels que le théâtre, les salons et les fêtes populaires d'Espagne, furent plagiées comme devant faire révolution dans la chorégraphie d'école française! En effet, elles y firent ressentir une influence pernicieuse. Si l'on traite un sujet de caractère espagnol, il est convenable de conserver la couleur locale, toujours avec un choix gardé par le bon goût; mais que la naïade et la duchesse, la bohémienne et l'écossaise, l'*Amour et Diane*, *Satanella* et la *Marguerite de Goëthe*, nous régalent à l'envi des frétillements de la *Madrilène*, cela doit sembler le comble de l'absurdité. Que voulez-vous? me diront les virtuoses dansantes, nous savons bien que ce genre est faux, insipide, révoltant même pour notre sentiment intime, mais cela fait de l'effet. Notre professeur le condamne, notre le directeur l'improuve, il l'exige même; cela fait pâmer d'aise les abonnés des baignoires et ces gants blancs donnent le signal à la machine infernale, placée sous le grand lustre. La salle est ébranlée d'applaudissements, de faux aloi il est vrai, mais le public est étourdi, et nous avons l'air d'être portées aux nues.

7 A sample from the printed French edition of August Bournonville's fourth letter, including his handwritten corrections and revisions for a planned collected edition in book form of his eight *Letters on Dance and Choreography*.

LETTERS ON DANCE
AND CHOREOGRAPHY

AUGUST BOURNONVILLE

THE FIRST LETTER

Copenhagen, 1860

Monsieur Ch. Desolme,
During my last journey to Paris this year, our conversations regarding the progress and the set-backs of theatrical dance, in relation to the other lyric and dramatic arts, inspired in you the desire to see assembled in a series of articles the observations which I have permitted myself to make on the present state of the ballet at the Imperial Academy of Music.[1]

On returning to my country retreat, where the summer vacation affords me the leisure to devote myself to the delights of reading, I have opened again, perhaps for the hundredth time, the *Lettres sur la danse et sur les ballets*, written by Noverre;[2] on each page of this remarkable book, one is struck by the light that this eminent artist sheds not only on the particular art of which he is a master, but on all the topics he encounters on his way. First of all, one is left, so to speak, enlightened by the deep and respectful love that he has devoted to his divine muse, that *light-footed Terpsichore*, who, thanks to his genius, he has been able to

---

[1] From its foundation in 1661 until this century the official name of the Paris Opéra Ballet was Académie Royale (later Impériale/Nationale) de Danse. The ballet at the Paris Opéra is now named Ballet du Théâtre National de Paris.

[2] Jean-Georges Noverre's *Lettres sur la danse et sur les ballets* was first published by Aimé Delaroche of Lyons in 1760, with a small number of copies published in Stuttgart. Bournonville's copy of this book (now in a private collection in Copenhagen) is the 1760 Stuttgart variant. It contains his pencilled annotations and other remarks in marginal notes.

reconcile with her more serious and eloquent sisters,[3] and to whom he erected altars, whose cult was long sustained through the following generations.

To know and appreciate the origin and the developments, the mechanism and the spirit of the dance as adapted to the stage by means of pantomime, one need only consult Noverre's book (editions of 1760, 1783, 1803 and 1807),[4] to find at the same time the names of those artists who have brought lustre to the dance at different periods.

Old routines were questioned and wounded pride led to an outcry of condemnation against the audacious reformer who, employed at the court of a German prince,[5] dared to disapprove of the customs adopted by the sublime Opéra de Paris. Nevertheless, it was not long before his influence began to be felt. . . . The masks, the panniers and the tonnelets, the feathered headdresses and the pointed heels disappeared, and the obsolete forms of the dance moved imperceptibly towards characterisation and dramatic situations.

Noverre, the regenerator of an art that since the time of Louis xiv had achieved a serious importance, became so famous that the foremost theatres in Europe quarrelled over him. He established a school in Vienna, and in that capital city he was able

[3] Bournonville here refers to the muses Thalia (the Muse of Comedy) and Melpomene (the Muse of Tragedy).
[4] Noverre's letters were published as follows: (1) in Lyon/Stuttgart by A. Delaroche, 1760 (484 pp.); (2) in Paris by A. Londres, 1783 (2nd edition, viii–368 pp.); (3) in St Petersburg, by J. C. Schnoor, 1803–04 (4 vols. of which vol. 3 contains the scenarios of his ballets); and (4) in Paris by L. Collin, 1807 (2 vols.). Moreover, an English translation was published in London, 1782–83 (by G. Robinson, 3 vols., of which vol. 3 contains the scenarios of his ballets). During the twentieth century a new French edition was published in Paris, 1927 (by Éditions Tourelle, iv–214 pp.) while a revised English edition was published in London, 1930 (by C. W. Beaumont, 170 pp.), and a new English translation was published by Cobbet Steinberg, 1980 (in *Dance Anthology*, New American Library).
[5] Between 1760 and 1768 Noverre was engaged as ballet-master at the court of the Duke of Württemberg, Stuttgart.

to put into practice his ideas on ballet d'action in such an impressive way that at Court and among the audience he enjoyed the reputation of a second Michelangelo, whose abruptness and arrogance he sometimes emulated.

French to the core, he could not resist the urge to shine on the stage of the Opéra, to which he was summoned by his royal patron, Marie-Antoinette,[6] to whom he had had the honour of giving lessons, and who procured for him all the power which a ballet-master could have at that time.

Nevertheless, the success of his compositions did not live up to the expectations of his admirers. The transition of Tircis and Phylis into the passionate movements of these historical characters was too abrupt for the Parisian public; the renowned *maître*, not having been able to bring with him the mimes from his school, had been obliged to use established soloists in the principal rôles who were unaccustomed to dramatic expression; finally, the masterpieces of the French theatre, transformed by Noverre into *tableaux mouvants*, mimed scenes and dancing crowds, far from having the same attraction in France as in those foreign countries where the pantomime was regarded as the best form of translation of words, produced in Paris nothing but indignation and derision. The latter reaction was the most frequent, and the first performed ballet, based on a tragedy by Corneille, the *Combat des Horaces et des Curiaces*, became the object of the most bitter pleasantries.[7]

[6] In August 1776 Noverre was called to Paris by Queen Marie-Antoinette who appointed him ballet-master at the royal court of France, a post he held until 1781.
 [7] Noverre's tragic ballet in five acts was named *Les Horaces* and was premièred at the Paris Opéra on 21 January 1777 to a score by Joseph Starzer. This ballet was assessed a century later by Théodor de Lajarte as follows: "The first idea for this ballet was indeed a real audacity. To comment in pantomime on a theme treated by the great Corneille could only be dared by Noverre. Anyhow, he had the good taste of not following the exact same scheme as that of the tragedy [. . .] At the first performance the Queen [Marie-Antoinette]

Like all great geniuses, Noverre achieved the glory of a martyr, but the ground that he had prepared was fertilised by his suffering. In France, the *Daubervals*, the *Gardels* and *Milon*;[8] in Italy the *Viganos* and *Gioja* benefited from the fruits of his labours;[9] but the name of Noverre, repeated continually, if not by his followers, at least by men of taste, hovered over all those choreographic works where *beauty* was united with *truth*, *poetry* with *logic*, and his name still seems to want to survive the dissolution that threatens an *art* which the present generation almost refuses to recognise as such.

Great confidence in the eternal feeling for Beauty, as well as in the forbearance of my readers, is needed in order to dare to take up once again a topic in which interest has considerably decreased, or rather whose ideas have moved in a contrary direction to their original source; courage is needed to defend a cause which, both because of its champions and its detractors, has come to be regarded as frivolous. Noverre's work of genius first appeared in 1760, and I admit that it requires a degree of au-

arrived accompanied by Madame and the Countess d'Artois with her sisters-in-law, in order to demonstrate their welcome to their protégé, Noverre. The audience, a little confused by this mimic work on Roman history, strongly applauded the artists [. . .] but only half-heartedly enjoyed the new ballet by Noverre, which achieved only seven performances. The *Journal de Paris* makes us understand that *Les Horaces* had already been performed in Vienna 'with great succes'." (*Bibliothèque musicale du théâtre de l'opéra*, Vol. I, Paris, Librarie des Bibliophiles, 1878; reprinted by Georg Olms Verlag, Hildesheim, 1969.)

[8] Among the greatest choreographers in French ballet during the late eighteenth and early nineteenth centuries were Jean Dauberval (b. Bercher, 1742–1806), Maximilien-Léopold-Philippe-Joseph Gardel (known as Gardel *aîné*, 1741–1787), Pierre Gabriel Gardel (1758–1840) and Louis Jacques Milon (1766–1849).

[9] The perhaps greatest late eighteenth century and early nineteenth century Italian choreographers were Salvatore Viganò (1769–1821) and Gaetano da Gioja (1764–1826).

dacity for a follower of modern choreography to seize the pen abandoned by the famous *maître*, whose style, so full of clarity and eloquence, deserved the praises of the philosopher from Ferney.[10] Nevertheless, it is my muse who summons me through the voice of the *past century*. I will follow my calling, I will obey my artistic conscience; if the passion which inspires me is not the fire of genius, may it at least be perceived as stemming from a sincere love, and if the letters that I sign are not destined to influence the future of ballet, may they at least serve to honour a memory and to fill a gap left open by Noverre's followers.

In spite of the limited number of those who have been able to profit from the precious lessons contained in the *Lettres sur la danse*, there will perhaps be some modern choreographers, of greater theatrical repute than I, who will dispute my right to aspire to be the successor to our common *maître*, and who will contradict my opinion regarding a branch of the arts which is diverging more and more from the needs of the stage in favour of gymnastics that are forced, lewd and ridiculous. I neither wish, nor can I enter into a sterile polemic, but I will try, in order to avoid any personal controversy, to address the effects and the causes, without drawing attention to the shortcomings of individuals.

Having myself danced, taught, written and composed, I may presume to expect some confidence on the part of colleagues, and if, happily, my letters are regarded as being sincere, especially if they do not seem all too devoid of interest, I hope to win the public to the cause which is so dear to me. As my services were not rejected by the Opéra's administration, nor my advice scorned by the dancers, I harbour none of the resentment against them so clearly implicit in Noverre's didactic writings – I

---

[10] Bournonville here refers to the great eighteenth-century French philosopher, François Marie Arouet de Voltaire, who lived in the town of Ferney (Gex) between 1760 and 1768.

do not wish to entertain the reader with descriptions of my own ballets; therefore I need not attempt to defend them; moreover, inspired by his example, I could, if necessary, invite devotees to come and see my works at the Royal Theatre of Copenhagen; but, in spite of my youthful enthusiasms and my vanity, I will refrain from presenting them on the stage of the French Opéra.

I will finish this letter by devoting a few lines to the memory of my *maître*, the celebrated Auguste Vestris [deceased in] (1843).[11]

This excellent artist, who, during a long and brilliant period, was the favourite of the Parisian public, whom he entertained with his joyful liveliness, was envied by many who tried to persuade his contemporaries to see him as a fool, a dandy, whose entire mind was in his legs. They even confused him with *Gaëtano Vestris*, his father, who, because of his affected lordly behaviour combined with his semi-Italian slang, provided piquant opportunities for derision.[12] From this curious mixture of characteristics, there emerged a notorious puppet-like figure who, more than once, I saw delivered to the ridicule of the boulevard public. – It is to this, then, that one of the brightest of all theatrical careers has been reduced!!!

Meanwhile, I ask my still active *chefs d'emploi*, my old classmates, and those dancers younger than I am who knew this extraordinary artist in his maturity or in his old age, has there ever been a better representative of French graciousness and urbanity in all the world? Lively, light-hearted, sensitive and

---

[11] Auguste Vestris (b. Marie-Jean-Augustin, 1760–1842) was Bournonville's private teacher during his long sojourns in Paris in the late 1820s, and probably represents the single most influential and lasting force on Bournonville's early choreographic ideals in dance style and technique. Vestris did not die in 1843, as stated by Bournonville, but on 5 December 1842.

[12] Gaëtan (or Gaëtano) Apollino Baldassare Vestris (1729–1808) worked as a dancer and choreographer at the Paris Opéra between 1749 and 1784, where he created several ballets in close collaboration with Noverre and Maximilien Gardel.

generous, he loved not only the dance and the theatre, but everything that was beautiful, spiritual and courteous. His fire warmed without burning anyone who approached him, for he was impetuous without rage, critical without malice, superior without arrogance. Gifted with a lively imagination and exquisite taste, he knew better than anyone how to reveal his pupils' qualities and to conceal their faults; and those who, by chance, understood how to grasp his advice, were often able to profit from it for the rest of their careers.

In the way he conceived dance, one could easily perceive the astonishing degree of execution which he must have possessed; but when he devoted himself to the play of pantomime, he was completely transformed. Were it l'*Enfant prodigue*,[13] *Télémaque*[14] or a completely different character, all were of a simmering youth, and one was overwhelmed with wonder facing an actor of the highest rank. He also used to say to us: What do you want me to teach you! Go to the Louvre, study antiquity, see *Talma*,[15] search out natural grace, admire *Mlle Mars*.[16] What man of spirit could express such a happy thought more eloquently!

And did his school consist of rigid pedantry or was it nothing but the echo of ancient traditions? *Vestris* was always a step ahead of the latest novelties, since he knew how to adopt them by giving them that aura of good taste which tended to be attributed to the air of Paris, but which was nothing other than the effect of his genius, an influence that, since his death, to our great

[13] *L'Enfant prodique*, a pantomimic ballet in three acts by Pierre Gardel set to a score composed and arranged by Henri Berton, was premièred at the Paris Opéra on 28 April 1812.
[14] *Télémaque dans l'ile de Calypso*, a heroic ballet in three acts by Pierre Gardel set to a score by E. L. Müller, was premièred at the Paris Opéra on 15 June 1790.
[15] François-Joseph Talma (1763–1826), perhaps the greatest French actor during the late eighteenth and early nineteenth centuries.
[16] Mlle Mars (b. Anne-Françoise-Hippolyte Boutet, 1779–1847), perhaps the greatest French actress in the late eighteenth and the first four decades of the nineteenth century.

regret, is no longer to be seen. It is to be hoped that this tribute, paid to the truth and to the reverence owed to the *maître*, will be supported by the witness of all those who knew him as an artist. He was more than a great talent, he was *truly a man*, and one of his most honourable qualities, which we cannot recommend enough to those who enjoy the favours of a fickle public, was the store of modesty with which he used to speak of his epoch, of his merits, and of his success.

My intention, within the following series of letters, is to deal with several interesting matters relating to the dance and the ballets at the Opéra, and I count on both your personal benevolence and your solicitude with regard to the gracious art that is the object of my studies and my worship.

AUGUST BOURNONVILLE

This first letter will be followed by five others that will deal with the following matters:
1 THE PROGRESS AND THE DECADENCE OF THE DANCE.
2 COMPOSITION AND CHOREOGRAPHY.
3 SCHOOL, EXERCISES, THEATRICAL EDUCATION.
4 CHARACTERS, COSTUMES.
5 THE FUTURE AND PROJECTS OF REORGANISATION.[17]

---

[17] Bournonville changed his original plan for only six articles at an early stage to the present series of eight articles as a result of his decision to divide the section that deals with "Composition and Choreography" into three separate letters.

THE SECOND LETTER

There is nothing more difficult than comparing artists who have graced the stage at different times. Nothing remains but tradition or a few ephemeral impressions; memories either fade away or assume fabulous dimensions, according to the character of those who transmit them; moreover, for young people the present is all, whereas old men dwell only in the past; serious analysis and fair judgement are hindered by the one group's disbelief and by the other's regrets and bitterness. Let us try to fall into neither of these extremes, and, aiming at nothing but the interest of an art which has charmed the leisure of our fathers and which will be a part of our children's honest pleasures, let us see if, among the shadows of this magic lantern, we are able to learn a salutary lesson.

In everything concerning the principles of the *danse d'école*, I would not add a single syllable to Noverre's reasoned treatise on the mechanics of *pas* and *attitudes*; this would not only be a superfluous task, but a waste of time, not having before me, as the famous *maître* had, a generation accustomed to regarding the dance as an essential part of chivalrous exercises and urbane manners. At the time when the last edition of the *Lettres sur la Danse* (1807) appeared,[1] the fashionable world and the ordinary people, the army and the bourgeoisie still applied themselves to a noble and dignified dance. The *Menuet*, the *Gavotte*, the *Alle-*

---

[1] See p. 24, note 4.

mande, and the *French Contredanse* required several years of good lessons,[2] and one could find at the Court of the First Empire some dilettantes who were as good at dancing as they are nowadays at playing the piano. It is therefore not surprising that, at that time, there were some connoisseurs capable of appreciating the value of accomplishments acquired through study and reflection. Today, it is otherwise: society hardly dances at all any more, and in order to be able to drag their legs nonchalantly along shiny dance floors, young people need no longer endure the rigours of practising *battements*; one is only too happy if *gymnastics* do not lead them to acquire a strong taste for tours de force and if the *public balls* do not push them into the shamelessness of the *cancan*.

As long as theatrical dance has existed, audiences have had their declared favourites, and the public and the *maîtres* have rarely agreed on the merits of first-rank artists. Whilst the professors were extolling the virtues of perfection of detail, the amateurs concerned themselves with the charm of the whole, demanding from talent nothing but the echo of their own feelings.

The *courtier* searched for nobility of manners; the *warrior*, for boldness and vigour; the *poet*, for the ideal and the nebulous; the *painter*, for plastic forms; the *musician*, for clear-cut rhythms; the *dramatic actor*, for the reflection of human passions and the expression of character; finally, the *philosopher*, for a logical combination of ideas.

One must admit that the opinions of an audience consisting

---

[2] The French *contredanse* was described by George Desrat in 1895 as a dance from the eighteenth century that consisted of a single set of movements and could be performed by an unlimited number of persons. It is classified by him as a dance with close similarities to the *cotillon*. However, while the *cotillon* later developed into the *quadrille*, the French *contredanse* remained a dance that did not necessarily have to be performed *vis-à-vis*, as is the case with the *quadrille* (see George Desrat, *Dictionnaire de la Danse*, Paris, Libraires-Imprimeries-Réunies, 1895).

of such people would essentially be the right ones. But, on the other hand, no artist would be able to meet all these requirements without having first surmounted the difficulties of a formal training.

The arts, like everything achieved in this world, require two actions: giving and receiving. It is not just a matter of *acting* a part, the audience must be able to understand and to feel; the *dance* needs an audience sensitive to true beauty. In an assembly of people such as the one I have just envisaged, there would be great potential for appreciation, even though this might not include an understanding of the specialised technique. But, as soon as what one expects from the theatre is nothing more than elaborate surprises, oddities of imagination, sloppy voluptuousness, bacchic joy, gross sensuality, delirium and insanity, then the fresh pleasures and the noble emotions, the frank joyfulness, the spirit, the poetry and the moral strength forsake the temple of the muses, and the *ballet*, reduced to a marketplace populated with odalisques, turns the Théâtre de l'Opéra into a sick and enfeebled man.

I intend to continue to examine the mutual influence which, in a big theatre, the stage and the auditorium exert on one another, and to establish which of these two is particularly responsible for either the progress or the decline of any art; only, I wish to stop for a moment to draw attention to the contrast which often prevails between the taste of an audience and the spirit of a *nation* or of the *times*.

In France, the reign the Sybarite and the periwig saw the birth of the strongest tragedies; the régime of the Terror rejoiced in promoting the pastorale and the sweet fictions of mythology. The *moral drama* flourished under the Directory, and the martial Empire was the cradle of sentimental romances.

Licentious vaudeville boomed under the pious and devoted Restoration; finally, the peaceful and wholly bourgeois period of the July government cultivated, with equal success, the frenzies of the first revolution, the mediaeval atrocities, and the crimes of the *Gazette des Tribunaux*.

After this survey of theatrical anomalies, I think that one would be wrong to expect, from the more or less flourishing state of the arts of the stage, consequences as serious for France as those which inflicted their degradations on the Oriental Empire. Nevertheless, one would not be wrong in regarding the existence of the theatre and of the special artistic genres as being seriously endangered and dragged along a fatal downward path, making it almost impossible to stop. Out of extravagance, indeed, are born distaste and aversion, and both lead to total annihilation. Furthermore, the motto of our days is: "*Après nous le déluge*."[3] This cry of indifference, with regard to art, injures the heart and crushes the ear of the true friend of that which is beautiful and good.

In my next letter, I will put aside the interests of the other branches of theatre to devote myself exclusively to the *dance* and to the progress it has achieved since Noverre ceased writing, which covers just about the period of half a century.

AUGUST BOURNONVILLE

---

[3] "After us, the flood", an idiom which suggests unconcern about what happens after we have gone.

THE THIRD LETTER

Social dancing, in its true form, no longer exists except as a dead language taught at school, useful to the development of youth, neglected in everyday life and based on the trivialities of galops and polkas. Therefore, if the *danse basse* – such was its academic name – can no longer learn anything from *theatrical dancing*, the latter, on the other hand, now has to do without those former models with which the court, the town, and popular festivals once provided it. The study of dance based on nature, especially in France, has almost totally ceased.

The inciting influence of Noverre's genius brought about a true revolution in dance which, until then, had been confined within very narrow limits. It became associated with the fine arts, with drama, and principally with the use of melody now released from its age-old restraints. The rigid forms of the *chaconne* and the *passepied* gave way to *pas expressifs* and to *scènes combinées*; these preserved the differences between the *genres* or distinctive categories which the dancers dared not abandon; but at the same time these dances required a flow of continuous movement allowing neither rest nor any differences of execution. The *pas à échos alternatifs*[1] were thus developed, giving the

---

[1] By this term Bournonville means a form of dance (ususally a *pas de deux*) which consists of a series of identical choreographic solos that are performed by the male and female dancer respectively, as if "echoing" each other. An outstanding example of this is the so-called *Pas de la Vestale* that is now part of the Bournonville School (Saturday's Class), but was originally created by Pierre Gardel as a divertissement in Gaspare Spontini's 1807 opera *La Vestale*.

eye the time to study their respective qualities; but there remained an uneven struggle so long as the heterogeneous nature of the sexes was ignored. Consequently, it became necessary to take into consideration the genre of each individual dancer, and each one knew how best to display separately the particular advantages of his or her talent. The vigorous, light, noble, or comic *danseurs* had their own phrases of music, and the gracious, lively, or piquant *danseuses* were placed according to their height and to the characteristics of their steps. These dances often had as introduction a short pantomime scene or an *adagio* of picturesque attitudes, but *group scenes* were very rarely used and had to be brought about by the dramatic situation. The *corps de ballet*, formerly arranged in lines along two lateral columns, served only to mark the *annonces* of the *grands pas* and had therefore acquired the honourable nickname of *coast-guard*. This battle order was maintained in the *contredanses* which formed the mandatory finale of the *ballets d'action* until the invention of the *quadrilles en ligne de front*.[2] The *diagonales* and *demi-cercles* came about only later, and the use of crowds, in a studied disorder, was a still later choreographic development. Nevertheless, in the days of our ancestors, just as today, no *maître de ballet* ever succeeded in involving and interesting the whole cast of *figurants* and *coryphées* at the Opéra in the action or in the poetry of the performance. The little conversations, the quick glances into the auditorium, the apathy displayed during scenes of enthusiasm, the witty remarks and the derisive laughter during tragic scenes, have always been a particular and distinctive feature of the corps de ballet at the Académie royale et impériale de musique.

In the period between 1807 and 1830 the most celebrated names in dance were, besides *Vestris* and *Duport*, Mmes *Gardel*,

[2] This term was used to describe a new kind of scenic variant of the *quadrille* in which all dancers performed *en ligne* towards the audience as if they were dancing with imaginary partners in the auditorium.

Clotilde and *Chameroy*, already mentioned by *Noverre*; – *Albert, Paul, Antonin, Ferdinand* and *Perrot*, Mmes *Bigottini, Gosselin, Fanny Bias* and *Montessu*.[3]

One can see from this list of dance celebrities that the reputation of the men was at least equal to that of the women; their success was naturally shared, since their energy, masculine elegance and polished schooling earned the audience's esteem for the *danseurs*; just as their flexibility, the *exquisite finish* of their execution, and their feminine grace, together with the heart's temptations, achieved, as they have always and everywhere, the triumph of the fair sex. It is certain that the above-mentioned epoch was one of real progress. This was due as much to the superior gifts of the leading figures of the day as to the abundance of secondary talents.

The arrival of *Mlle Marie Taglioni* (1827) heralded a new era for the dance at the Opéra. This excellent dancer had an expression of innocence, a youthful freshness that, without inspiring voluptuousness, charmed the heart with endless pleasure. She was a real sylph, a daughter of the waves, a virtuous maiden, a young lady of good family, in short everything that can be imagined as pure, gracious and poetic, combined with a talent whose outstanding quality was an airy lightness. It gave great satisfaction, both to the professional and to the amateur, to see her appear on stage, since the former was happy that he too professed such a charming art, and the latter was struck by a

---

[3] The dancers listed here are: Auguste Vestris (b. Marie-Jean-Augustin, 1760–1842), Louis-Antoine Duport (known as Duport *aîné*, 1781/1783–1853), Marie-Elisabeth Anne Gardel (b. Houbert, also known as Mlle Miller, 1770–1833), Clotilde-[Augustine Malfleuret] (1793–1819), Adrienne Chameroy (1779–1802), Albert (stage name for François Decombe, 1787–1865), Antoine Paul (known as *l'Aërien*, 1798–1871), Antonin (nineteenth century), Ferdinand (stage name for Jean La Brunière de Médicis, 1791–1837), Jules Joseph Perrot (1810–1892), Emilie Bigottini (1784–1858), Constance Hippolyte Gosselin (m. Anatole, 1794–?), Fanny Bias (1789–1825), Pauline Montessu (b. Paul, 1805–1877).

poetry he had not previously thought it possible to find in dance; finally, she represented to me the living image of *Terpsichore*, in spite of the imperfections that more malevolent eyes than mine took the trouble to try to find in her. The finest praise of her, and thus of her profession, was expressed by a serious old gentleman who, on his way to a performance by the famous dancer, told me in passing: "Sir, I am going to the Opéra to have a lesson in good taste."

That was a time of brilliance for *dance* and for *song*. The classic and modern opera had as performers *Nourrit*, *Dérivis père*, *Levasseur* and *Dabadie*, Mmes *Cinti*, *Dabadie* and *Mori*.[4] It was the happy season of *Auber* and *Rossini*, and it seemed to be springtime again for the ballet, borne on the breeze of gracefulness animating the steps of our new *Psyché*,[5] since everybody, audience and artists alike, acknowledged that the charm of the dance did not consist of impressions of astonishment, but of a divine harmony which, to the spirit of gesture and movement, is what its delicious fragrance is to the rose.

The confrontations and rivalries ceased of their own accord, and a noble emulation now surrounded the pretended innovator who, in her sweet modesty, knew better than anyone that she represented nothing but an ancient and immutable truth.

At this time, the government still looked particularly favourably on the Opéra which, in spite of the abuses seemingly inseparable from this kind of institution, still merited the glorious title of *Académie*. The absolutism and the corruption of the

---

[4] The singers listed here are: Adolphe Nourrit (1802–1839), Henri-Etienne Dérivis (known as Dérivis père, 1780–1856), Nicolas (Prosper) Levasseur (1791–1871), Henri-Bernard Dabadie (1797–1853), Laure (Cinthie) Cinti-Damoreau (b. Montalant, 1801–1863), Louise Dabadie (b. Zulme Leroux, 1804–1877), Mlle Mori (m. Gosselin, nineteenth century).

[5] Bournonville refers here to Marie Taglioni (1804–1884), who was often described by her contemporaries as the personification of the mythological figure of Psyche after she had performed the title-rôle in Pierre Gardel's pantomimic ballet of that name at the Paris Opéra on 23 February 1829.

premiers sujets à recette,[6] the pre-arranged *adulation*, the publicity, the curtain calls, and finally the showers of wreaths and bunches of flowers, were not yet known. It is characteristic of constitutional regimes to provide theatres with the *absolute power* of subsidised directors and impresarios, as is the case in Italy, who then take advantage of the public's enthusiasm while exhausting the artists' popularity, with the laudable aim of retiring as millionaires.

AUGUST BOURNONVILLE

---

[6] This term was used for the soloists or demi-soloists who, by contract, were paid only with a percentage of the box office receipts each night.

THE FOURTH LETTER

(continued)

As a result of the new system of administration of subsidised theatres, the Opéra ceased to be an artistic institution and simply became a *business*. With a sharp speculator put in charge, it was not long before the consequences of the principle adopted by all such secondary enterprises, that is the isolation of the first rank of artists, began to be felt.

As both the quality of the ensemble and the rivalry between talented artists were considered to be superfluous, they were replaced by luxurious stage properties. The future of theatre having become, so to speak, a matter of little consequence, all that now mattered was to concentrate on impressive effects, on exciting the audience's curiosity . . . on making money. In order to do that, it was necessary to place as much emphasis as possible on one individual, on a goose that lays golden eggs – but one that can be replaced according to the duration and the whims of current fashion.

The extraordinary success of Mlle Taglioni contributed admirably to this system; her name printed on the poster was then enough to fill the auditorium; all rivalry was considered dangerous since it could distract attention from the principal object, and soon the famous artist was surrounded by nothing but female dancers who were more or less *figurantes*, and a very limited number of male dancers. The lonely and incomparable goddess soon experienced the inconstancy of her fans when a new star appeared in the person of Fanny Elssler, arriving from Vienna, cradle of the talent of the unequalled sylph, and surrounded by an historic mystery that, for a certain type of amateur, was a further attraction.[1]

The genre of Fanny Elssler was undoubtedly less pure, less perfect than that of Marie Taglioni, but it was at the time suited to those ideas which, in spite of sound teaching, had invaded the domain of the arts in general, and that of the dance in particular.

Taglioni's dancing was essentially *chaste*, that of Elssler exuded and inspired *voluptuousness*. A witty critic compare the one to a blue sky, the other to a bright red one. It was really the difference between the north and the south, Jenny Lind and Malibran, Thorwaldsen and Canova.[2] The former had transported dance into ethereal regions; the latter led it into the warm climate of Mahomet's paradise. With Taglioni, one forgot the theatre and this base world; with Elssler, one risked forgetting everything. Indeed, the misty creations of the sylph with transparent wings vanished amid the clatter of the *Gipsy* tambourine.[3] It was as if the forgetful audience had been bitten by *La Tarentule*;[4] they let themselves be bewitched by *La Chatte*

---

[1] The "historic mystery" to which Bournonville refers was a skilfully publicised hint of a romantic love affair between Fanny Elssler (1810–1884) and the Duke of Reichstadt, Napoleon's son and heir, who, after his death in 1832 in the flower of his youth, had become a martyr in the growing Napoleonic legend (*see* Ivor Guest, *Fanny Elssler*, London, 1970).

[2] The four Northern and Southern European artists listed here are the Swedish soprano Jenny Johanna Maria Lind (m. Goldschmidt, 1820–1887), the Spanish soprano Maria-Felicia Malibran (b. Garcia, 1808–1836), the Danish sculptor Bertel Thorvaldsen (1768/1770–1844), and the Italian sculptor Antonio Canova (1757–1822).

[3] *La Gipsy*, a pantomimic ballet in three acts and five tableaux to a score by François Benoist, Ambroise Thomas and Aurelio Marliani, was premièred at the Paris Opéra on 28 January 1839. It was in this ballet that Elssler performed her famous Polish solo *La Cracovienne*.

[4] *La Tarentule*, a pantomimic ballet in two acts by Jean Coralli set to a score by Casimir Gide, was premièred at the Paris Opéra on 24 June 1839.

métamorphosée en Femme,[5] and totally lost their heads at the sound of the *Cachucha* castanets.[6] This idealised Spanish dance was a landmark in the annals of ballet at the Opéra. Inserted into a scene of *Le Diable boiteux*, it determined the success of that entire work. Her elegant figure, her delicious abandon, and most of all the beautiful dancer's shining eyes, lent an inebriating charm to this *pas seul*, which by its ease, and even its brevity, led to repeated *encores* and aroused an enthusiasm close to delirium. It was, so to speak, a battle of love between the actress and the spectator, who, thinking of himself as the only one favoured among the crowd, would have hated any man performing at her side as the object of her coquetry. All this imaginary jealousy was perfectly well understood by Fanny, and in order to reassure her worshippers, she created special engagements for her sister Thérèse,[7] a skilful and correct dancer, but whose [bodyguard] stature distanced her from the category of nymphs and shepherdesses. This faithful sister devoted herself entirely to the service and the successes of her younger sibling; she supported her in their groupings, filled in any gaps, resigned herself to the audience's coolness, and even condescended to dress as a man so as to withhold any masculine attention from the enchantress.

The banishment of male dancers started at this time, and the press justified their support for this measure by citing and ridiculing the imperfections of certain persons who were held up as

[5] *La Chatte metamorphosée en femme*, a ballet in three acts and seven scenes by Jean Coralli set to a score by Alexandre de Montfort, was premièred at the Paris Opéra on 16 October 1837.
[6] *La Cachucha* was perhaps Fanny Elssler's most famous Spanish solo dance. It was premièred as an interpolated number in Jean Coralli's three-act pantomimic ballet *Le Diable boiteux*, set to a score by Casimir Gide and premièred at the Paris Opéra on 1 June 1836.
[7] Thérèse Elssler (1808–1876) arranged several of her younger sister's solos and also choreographed a pantomimic ballet for her entitled *La Volière, ou Les Oiseaux de Boccace*. It was set to a score by Casimir Gide and premièred at the Paris Opéra on 5 May 1838.

typical examples of the genre. No sooner had a sufficient number of *ladies* been found who were ready to renounce the bashful graces of their sex, than the *shepherds*, *major-domos*, *hussars* and *musketeers* ceased to be represented other than in the guise and form of young ladies, and the *gentlemen*, reduced to walk-on parts or supernumeraries, performed only in the most urgent cases and as an unavoidable inconvenience; they were indeed only too thankful not to be obliged to rig themselves out in women's clothing in order to complete the confusion and upset any dramatic illusion.

A century earlier several important Italian theatres, not considering the dance to be an occupation suitable to the dignity of the fair sex, had young boys dance dressed as women; perhaps it is there that the *affectation*, the *décolleté* of certain Italian dancers comes from, but in the period to which I now refer the opposite extreme seems to have prevailed. The art of dance being regarded as nothing more than an appeal to sensuality, and having thus descended to the level of oriental divertissements, was declared incompatible with the character of any serious and reasonable man, and the notion of a *harem* naturally excluded any kind of male rivalry. Thus the prevailing clique were unsparing in their persecution and moral destruction of an honourable category of artists who, as regards performing, and even teaching and composition, constitute an irreplaceable element of a branch of the theatre which, at that time, gloried in the boast of French supremacy.

Dancing men were jeered at and humiliated to such a degree that the consequences were felt well beyond the limits of the theatre, since young men who did not wish to refrain from the pleasures of dancing began to parody it with hideous and obscene contortions which, in the eyes of foreigners, constitute to this very day the national dance of the elegant Frenchman.

Of all Fanny Elssler's artistic productions, none achieved the popularity of *la Cachucha*, and her triumph reached its climax in front of the Spanish audience of Havana.

This was the signal for a general invasion of *Bailadores* from the peninsula. To please Europe's different populations, eagerly awaiting piquant sensations, they stressed the impudence of their already rather lascivious dances so that they became unrecognisable even to the eyes of Spaniards, and I am convinced that the compatriots of *Calderon* and *Murillo*[8] must have blushingly disavowed these outrages, which resemble those wines to which a strong dose of alcohol has been added for the satisfaction of blasé palates. By going further and further they reached a degree of licentiousness impossible to describe without descending into cynicism.

Nevertheless, these so-called national dances, which one would have searched for in vain in honest places, such as Spain's theatres, refined social circles and popular festivals, were considered destined to revolutionise the choreography of the French school! In fact, they influenced it in a pernicious way. If one is treating a subject of Spanish character, it is appropriate to preserve its local colour, yet guided always by good taste in one's choice; but that the naiad, and the duchess, the bohémienne and the Scots woman, the *Amour et Diane*, *Satanella*, and *Marguerite* by Goëthe should entertain us with the wrigglings of the *Madrilène*, must surely be the pinnacle of absurdity. What do you want? the dancing female virtuosos will ask me; we are well aware that this genre is false, tasteless and even disgusting, but it is effective. Our teachers condemn it, but the director approves and even demands it; it makes the regular subscribers faint from satisfaction, and their white gloves give the signal to the infernal machine, from their seats under the big chandelier. The auditorium trem-

---

[8] The two seventeenth-century Spanish artists listed here are the writer Don Pedro Calderon de la Barca Henao y Riaño (1601–1687) and the painter Bartolomé Estéban Murillo (1618–1682).

bles with applause, not really genuine it's true, but the audience is stunned, and we feel we are being transported to the clouds.

The following day, we can read the praise given to our curvaceous forms, to the fire of our glances, to the passion of our movements. We are compared to fauns, to panthers, and to all the animals of the *Jardin des Plantes*. The bacchantes and the *Phrynés* from Athens are our sisters, and our names grace the most beautiful fillies at the Chantilly horse races. Our dance is called an ode to I know not which God of mythology; all the same, we must be pleased that we profess an art that is so dignified and appreciated.

As the Parisian school has renounced the delivery of *étoiles de premier ordre* to the Opéra, it remains only for me to record the triumphs of a long series of celebrities emanating from the conservatoires of Naples and Milan, who, in turn, have occupied the absolute throne of the French Terpsichore. I can do justice to the muscular strength and to the lung power of these stouthearted daughters of Italy; I would [even] speak about their beautiful black eyes if the continuous whirlwind of their spinning dances did not prevent me from admiring them at my ease; I am astonished at the sight of gymnastics which suggest an energy unknown to the rest of the feminine sex, and which is achieved, it is true, at the expense of that naïve grace which must be the hall-mark of all the arts, but I am seized by a deep melancholy when I consider that theatrical dance, which should march in the front line together with the finest scenic productions, finds itself here face to face with the wonders of the *Cirque* and of the trampoline! because, as soon as we aspire to dazzle the senses, we are humiliated and vanquished in the face of the juggler's agility and strength.

I leave it to the distinguished talents of the day to decide to what extent they may themselves be to blame for those criticisms I believe it my right to bestow on modern dancing. I will avoid personalities, since I feel that even the mildest criticism could hurt their artistic susceptibility; I wish, on the contrary, to be useful to them, without causing the least offence. For the rest, as my praises would not be able to add anything to existing reputations, nor be able to deal with all the critics' reasonings, I will restrict myself to dedicating a few lines to the memory of the creator of the rôles *dansomanes* of Giselle, Paquita and Mazourka.[9]

Carlotta Grisi was, as regards refinement of performance, the most perfect female dancer I have ever seen: with a little less distinctiveness and ideality than *Taglioni* and *Elssler*, she possessed to an equal extent the lightness, the verve and the qualities of schooling of her celebrated predecessors, and as for musical precision – if I am allowed to use this metaphor – she seemed to be riding a keyboard. Every note a step. Her expression was one of unreserved joy; she looked as if she were dancing just for her own pleasure.

If one were to compare the miming talents of the three dancing celebrities that I have just mentioned, I would say that *Marie Taglioni* identified completely with her rôles, *Fanny Elssler* was marvellously able to adapt them to her own individuality, and *Carlotta Grisi* put them at the service of her lively and joyful dancing.

An artist of a previous epoch must take great care not to criticise unfairly. If we were to agree on one point, it would be that ideal beauty has never been attained, maybe even less in dance than in any other field. Nevertheless, it is the duty of the dance, as it is its nature, to aim towards this noble goal, and we

---

[9] The three rôles to which Bournonville refers here were all created at the Paris Opéra by the Neapolitan-born ballerina, Carlotta Grisi (1819–1899). The first two were title-rôles in *Giselle, ou les Wilis* (premièred on 28 June 1841) and *Paquita* (premièred on 1 April 1846), while the third (*Mazourka*) belongs to Joseph Mazilier's two-act pantomimic ballet *Le Diable à quatre* (set to a score by Adolphe Adam and premièred on 11 August 1845).

must persuade ourselves of the truth that, when we prefer quantity to quality, inebriation of the senses to heart-felt pleasure, noisy acclamations to motivated approvals, we will get further and further away from this goal.

I do not believe I am wrong when I stress the erroneous direction that an art – formerly much honoured – has taken, and until I see performing skills connected to dramatic characterisation and equally divided between artists of both sexes, until I find in male dancers a masculine inspiration, and until the title of an *excellent dancer* is not in opposition to that of a *graceful woman*, I may be allowed to restrain my admiration and, instead, to turn my glance towards better times in the past and in the future.

AUGUST BOURNONVILLE

THE FIFTH LETTER

(continued)

The aim of this correspondence being to consider the question of choreography in relation to the Paris Opéra, without regard to foreign theatres, I may, in principle, forbear to consider the latter or to speak of the merits of the ballet-masters in the other European capitals. Moreover, Italy and Spain having left their mark on French dance, and with England taking advantage of the horse-racing season to draw all the celebrities to the steeple chases, there would not be anything new and interesting other than in St Petersburg, Berlin, Copenhagen and Warsaw – the Vienna [ballet] having lost much of its previous worth; but such a description would exceed the limits of the task that I have assigned to myself, and might even deter me from it, and since I am not aiming at making comparisons either more or less favourable to l'Académie impériale de musique, I intend to go to the very source of an evil which threatens to banish the *dance* forever from the domain of the arts.

Both in a positive and in a negative way, Europe will never be freed from the influence of *Paris*. It may protest, claim, condemn, but it will always finally yield to the decrees of despotic and capricious fashion; and in its futile despair, it inevitably succumbs to exaggeration.

The ballet is just like everything else: if in *Paris* they show signs of neglecting the action, they will abolish it completely abroad; if they reduce the number of male dancers, down there they will allow only female dancers; if the French newspapers declare the cult of Terpsichore to be useless, the foreign newspapers will resort to derision or punishment; so if a friend of truth and beauty hopes to win the day, if he wishes to make one last effort at avoiding imminent destruction, it is in Paris that the reaction will have to take place.

I do not put myself forward as an oracle, or as a tutor, or as a doctor-saviour in the face of a branch of the theatre which still enjoys considerable affection, but I am one who *points things out*, inconvenient and superfluous for some people, but useful and welcome, I hope, for all those who see something more than a frivolous amusement in the art of the stage.

The term *choreography* has in a peculiar way changed meaning since Noverre's times; today it is used equally with regard to composition and to performance, and the appellation of choreographer is lightly given to the least supernumerary, who transmits what he has seen either his chief or the youngest dancers doing, and for the most part in a rather imperfect form. If you consult the old dictionary of l'Académie,[1] you will find, in the explanation of the word, that the difference between dance and *choreography* is just as profound as that between agriculture and *geography*; and if you compare the inventor of a ballet with a door to door salesman or a self-styled *arranger*, you will have found the distance existing between the author of a book and the typographic editor.

Let us begin by dealing with choreography in the literal sense of this word and afterwards with what is now conven-

[1] See *Recueil de planches de L'Encyclopédie par ordre de matières. Tome Huitième*, Paris, Panckoucke, 1790. Planches 1–2 (*Chorégraphie ou Art d'écrire la danse*), and the entry *Chorégraphie* (pp. 383–395).

tionally called choreography, that is the composition of ballets and dances.

Noverre, in giving us some strange details about the history of choreography, objected strongly to any kind of annotations intended to record dance combinations or pantomime on paper. He persisted in seeing in these nothing but indecipherable scrawls, a hindrance to the spirit of imagination and a way of facilitating slavish copying; but he closed his eyes to the advantages which that science afforded composers, namely the means with which to avoid the hazards of improvisation, and to assist an unfaithful memory when reviving a work, or when altering rôles and steps. A great number of *maîtres de ballet* still follow Noverre's principle, the only one they have adopted. With no previous preparation, they arrive on the stage or in the rehearsal room; there they await inspiration and try to put their ideas in order, while the corps de ballet hangs about for hours, yawning, joking or sometimes testing the outbursts of temper of the troubled thinker, the unhappy improviser.

Gardel, Henry[2] and other outstanding choreographers always had their choreographic notes to hand, either in the form of sketches or in French technical terminology. With these *maîtres*, it was sufficient to show some evidence of intelligence; the lesson was sometimes strenuous and difficult, but it was always interesting and fertile; precision and speed were of the utmost importance, and both the author and the performer shared the pleasure of seeing a work of talent taking shape.

In my opinion it is this which can be demanded of choreography when applied to the stage, and if the artists can agree on a terminology for the dance vocabulary, they will be able to transmit gestures, steps and figures to their pupils or their friends, and

[2] The two French choreographers and ballet-masters listed here are Pierre Gabriel Gardel (1758–1840) and Louis-Xavier-Stanislas Henry (1784–1836).

it will be of help to all of those whose skill is not underpinned by a talent for invention.

My celebrated colleague, M. de Saint-Léon, has displayed in a profound work a most ingenious discovery, by which, without the help of any terminology, he notates all the dance steps by assigning different symbols to the arms and the legs, so that one can send a choreographic work to the most distant country, without worrying about not knowing the language, – but provided that a knowledge of *sténo-chorégraphie* is to be found there.[3] But therein lies the problem, since, in spite of the acclaimed speed of the method, it takes twenty times as long to decipher and grasp these notations than it takes to put them on paper; – which is just the opposite of with written music.

The fact is that, even if we could engrave our ballets in bronze, we could not assume a universal welcome for them.

Let us try, instead, to master and proclaim the eternal truths which must connect our art to poetry, and if our epoch is not allowed to fulfil the ideals of purity and nobility which lie at the heart of the theatre, let us, at least, leave the door open to progress.

Talent in composition applies normally to three genres: *le pas*, *le divertissement* and *le ballet d'action*.

Le pas is to choreography (in the modern meaning) what bravura singing is to the lyric drama, and the theme and varia-

---

[3] Arthur Michel Saint-Léon (1821–1870), the French choreographer and ballet-master, published in his main theoretical treatise on dance notation in 1852, entitled *La Sténochorégraphie, ou l'art d'écrire promptement la danse; avec biographies et portraits des plus célèbres maîtres de ballets anciens et modernes* (Paris, St Petersburg, Imp. Bertauts, 1852, 32 pp. including illustrations, music, choreographic notation and diagrams). In 1997 it was republished by Ramond Lister (Deighton Bell Ltd, Cambridge, 1997).

tions to the concerto. The artist displays all his skills therein; it is the focal point for the applause accorded to a principal rôle; it is the very meaning of existence for those whose talent is essentially ornamental.

I have already described the history of the *pas* such as it developed at the Opéra up to the arrival of *Mlle Taglioni*, who absorbed, so to speak, all the interest in herself alone. *Perrot*, together with *Carlotta Grisi*, still upheld the honour of the *pas de deux* which, under the direction of this excellent artist, developed in a very characteristic way. After that, things degenerated to the point where no one cared any longer about adapting the dances to the dramatic situation or to the subject matter of the ballet; whether related to a court feast or a Flemish *kermesse*, to the time of Francis I or Numa Pompilius, be it at the top of a mountain or at the doors of hell, one would see a half-naked woman arrive together with a man in a waistcoat and bathing trunks; the female dancer all a-glow and handing out kisses on the wing, the male dancer displaying his good taste by assuming as sullen an air as possible. The pas begins. The opera glasses are trained on the *prima ballerina*, who, with a series of poses, dazzles her admirers. The male dancer approaches her, nervously extending an arm to support his beauty, whilst standing, kneeling, as a gladiator, as a clown, in a series of groups, as she hovers on tiptoe on one foot. He lifts his ballerina, places her on his leg, on his hip, even on his shoulders, and all this only to let her fall back again, stupefied and exhausted, in positions which would be of extreme indecency if she were not, on the one hand, looking perfectly ridiculous, and on the other, worthy of inspiring the deepest pity.

The *allegretto* is begun by the female dancer, giving her a little respite from the tortures of the *adagio* and saving herself for her *variations*. It is in truth the only moment when one can see the dance suited both to the character of the music and to that of the woman; and the moderate success of the final phrase brings one back into the domain of sanity.

The *danseur*, who up to this moment has only performed as a *support*, now becomes an *odd-job man*; he fills in the gap needed in order to let the female virtuoso catch her breath, and it is with a series of tours de force performed *en manège*, repeated incessantly and ending with a *pirouette de grand cousin*,* that he completes his duty. Then comes the grand variation, in which all the difficulties are concentrated, and with which she demonstrates superior ability together with incredible boldness; but this will not suffice to arouse the enthusiasm of the glittering phalanx of admirers unless, at the end of her solo, the *danseuse* starts spinning as if she were trying to hide her pretty form with her skirt, and unless she ends kneeling and imploring the audience. The *recalls* follow one after the other, the *pas* lasts a quarter of an hour, and usually ends with a *galop*, often accompanied by a military band which marches onto the stage with ophicleide and bass drum, regardless of period or location.

The triumphant female artist ends with an *exit pose* in her faithful supporter's arms. The *bravos* explode, but not loud enough. The group is suddenly transformed by an arm movement, which sends the ballerina's head down to the level of her cavalier's knee, whilst the tip of her foot now points heavenwards. – Then the auditorium collapses from the applause, the air trembles with fanatical screams; the ballerina, called back several times, steps in front of the proscenium curtain, dragging her unassuming partner by the hand, and departs loaded with wreaths and bunches of flowers.

This kind of spectacle is not, as many would imagine, the product of the spontaneous inspiration of the performers, but

---

* A fast turn on the heel (of no great difficulty), characteristic of the dance performed by the obligatory fools in comic ballets of the past.

quite the opposite; indeed it is the fruit of a collaboration organised with the greatest care. What a result!

I remember having seen a scene sketched by Perrot's masterly hand (who, in my opinion, was wrong in applying it to the seduction scene of *Marguerite* by *Faust*);[4] it was the representation of the *seven deadly sins*. Well! The lascivious poses intended to portray lewdness could be regarded as *modesty* compared with the self-styled anacreontic groups which are the essence of the *pas de deux* – *noble* and *serious* – of our time.

It seems that the eye can become accustomed to any kind of extravagance; but when, after some years of absence, one hears the ovations that admirers squander on them, and even the excuses made for this lack of restraint, one feels particularly humiliated and ready to curse a life devoted to a profession that has reached this degree of degradation.

AUGUST BOURNONVILLE

[4] Jules Perrot's three-act ballet *Faust* (set to music by Hector Panizza) was originally created for Fanny Elssler at La Scala, Milan, in 1848. Bournonville attended a performance of it at Vienna's Kärnthnerthor Theatre in the late spring or early summer of 1854, prior to his tenure there as ballet-master in 1855–56. He described the scene of the Seven Deadly Sins rather ironically in his memoirs as follows: "One of the trials which poor Gretchen had to endure was the influence of the Seven Deadly Sins personified. The seventh and last of these winsome apparitions was Sloth, and it cannot be denied that it left its mark on the ballet's prima donna [Lucile Grahn]; though I must admit that she possessed an iron strength and staying power which probably deserved to be put to better use." (*My Theatre Life*, trans. from the Danish by Patricia N. McAndrew, Middletown, Conn., Wesleyan University Press, 1979, p. 217.)

THE SIXTH LETTER

(continued)

The *divertissement de danse*, as a feature of the lyric theatre of Paris, had its most brilliant period under Gardel. The triumphant celebrations of dancing in *la Vestale*, in *les Danaïdes*, in *Trajan*, in *Fernand Cortés*, and in *la Lampe merveilleuse*[1] were considered to be masterpieces in their genre, and contributed significantly to the great success of these operas, because they flowed directly from the dramatic situation, to which they were inextricably linked. It is otherwise with the majority of the divertissements added to or even imposed on the works of our modern composers. It is all too clear nowadays that it has been necessary to interrupt the action to make way for the frivolities of the ballet troupe's entrance, performing its usual exercises. This does nothing but impede the flow of the work, which is sometimes already moving rather slowly; or else it diverts the audience's attention to such a degree that, when the principal artists, after half an hour or more of silence, resume their places

---

[1] These five operas were all composed for the Paris Opéra, with divertissements by Pierre Gardel either for the première or for later restagings. They are: (1) Gasparo Spontini's three-act lyrical tragedy *La Vestale* (premièred on 16 December 1807); (2) Antonio Salieri's five-act lyrical tragedy *Les Danaïdes* (premièred on 26 April 1784, restaged in 1817), (3) Louis-Luc Persuis and Jean-François Lesueur's three-act lyrical tragedy *Le Triomphe de Trajan* (premièred on 23 October 1807); (4) Spontini's three-act opera *Fernand Cortez, ou la Conquête du Mexique* (premièred on 28 November 1808); (5) Nicolo Isouard's three-act fairy-opera *Aladin, ou La Lampe merveilleuse* (premièred on 6 February 1822 with a score completed by A.-M. Benincori and F.-A. Habeneck).

to begin singing again, the audience tries in vain to remember why they are there at all.

Such secondary embellishments are just like the profusion of scenery and the exaggerated luxury of the staging: they engage the eye at the expense of the musical effect. One can only approve the simplicity of the spectacle in operas of Italian origin. In these the singing, and sometimes even the dramatic acting, have pride of place; but one does not go to see them in order to wax ecstatic over the gifts of the female dancers, the painters, the stage mechanics, the costumiers and so on; one does not go to see them in order to be dazzled by the rays of an electric sunrise or fascinated by the sound of a real waterfall.

Several modern authors have dreamt of a future based on the amalgamation of the combined resources of drama, opera and ballet.[2] I believe, without any presumption, that I can foresee the fate of Babel awaiting this mixture of means. Let us have the same aims, agree mutual methods of instruction, thrust aside all narrow-minded jealousies, but let us avoid fusion, and with the arts, as with fine wines, let us not blend them.

I am aware that the system of divertissements means more than just a matter of economics for the administration as well as for the artist. It gives the latter the opportunity of being frequently employed; he earns his *feu*[3] without too much effort and without taxing his imagination. The director understands that with the development of ballet as a purely decorative form of entertainment, the *ballet d'action* will eventually disappear completely, and with this genre reduced as it is to a mere frame for a certain number of *pas* (of the kind I have just mentioned), the employment of several choreographers would no longer

[2] Bournonville here seems to refer in particular to Richard Wagner's *Oper und Drama*, first published by J. J. Weber in Leipzig in 1852.

[3] The *feu* was a system of extra pay for those dancers who participated in a number of performances that was higher than that actually demand by their contract.

seem necessary, resulting in considerable savings on the cost of each new production.

We now reach the important point, central to my topic, the kind of lyric drama in which the instrumental music lends its voice to the gestures and the steps, preventing them from being a *language of dumb signs*; a spectacle understood by the deaf and the inhabitants of distant lands, by old men and children, by the intelligent and the ignorant; the kind of expressive moving picture which would disturb the rhythm of a play or an opera, and for which the use of words would not suffice.

Here I shall have to concentrate my thoughts, so as not to find that I have enough material for an entire volume. Thus I will not mention all the historical concepts dealt with by Noverre, likewise all the critical remarks which the modern repertory has elicited from the feuilletons of the French press.

The *ballet d'action* is the true school of expressive pantomime; of motivated and meaningful dance; it is where the dancer is formed into a true artist.

This genre, placed in between drama and opera, borrows from the one in order to lend to the other. Less hindered by the *unities*[4] and free from the limits of language, it is closer to the study of nature, more accessible to people of different nationalities than all the competing arts; and wherever the movement of crowds and machinery is involved it reigns supreme.

There are subjects for ballet in which the dance, expressing joy, love and the imaginary nature of symbolic or fanciful beings, dominates as a dramatic element; there are others in which it only forms part of the action in the guise of a festive embellishment.

Wherever the story and the plot develop and unfold naturally, the pantomime becomes simple, easy and effective. I refer

---

[4] A reference to the three unities of time, place and action, stemming from Aristotle, and important in French classical drama.

you to the description that Noverre gives of Garrick's sublime talent.[5] But any conversation or dialogue in the form of conventional gestures will inevitably border on the ridiculous and will become incomprehensible to the great majority of the audience. Those unfortunate *placards* on rocks, on temples, or the *banners* explaining the action or the story belong to the infancy of the arts, and must be banned from the theatre as they are from picture galleries.

In spite of the difficulty there would always be in finding some *phoenix*, such as Noverre requires, to fulfil the functions of *maître de ballet*, it must be admitted that this profession requires something more than the ability to set the turns and leaps of a *pas*, or to arrange a galaxy of young ladies in rows for a contredanse: besides the basic knowledge, taste and imagination necessary to compose a ballet in which one can find some historical, poetic or moral meaning, the choreographer, like the author of any other genre, must be observant, willing to search, and brave enough to reject that which is superfluous.

The *maître de ballet* must make it a point of honour to devise the plans or libretti for his ballets himself. If he lacks the inventiveness needed to connect the various aspects of his composition dramatically, it can then no longer be said to be his own. I do not argue against the merit of a possible collaboration; but the choreographer who only composes according to a given programme is no more advanced than the musician who only orchestrates others' melodies, or the mason who rough-hews the marble for the sculptor, or the craftsman who illuminates an artist's images; he is like a hen who hatches out a duck's eggs.

Once this principle has been established, the art of choreo-

---

[5] David Garrick (1717–1779), perhaps the greatest English actor during the mid-eighteenth century. Bournonville's father, Antoine Bournonville, studied with him in London during his youth and was a great admirer of Garrick's talent for mimic expression.

graphy must soon break with most of today's ballet composers and arrangers. I can still see the fine creations of *Gardel*, *Milon*, *Didelot*, *Aumer* and *Albert* in my mind's eye,[6] and I wonder why *la Sylphide*, by Taglioni père, is the last ballet performed at the Opéra which was truly of the choreographer's *own invention* (one still finds those who wish to attribute its programme to another great artist). Anyway, here is a ballet, at least in its original version, in which the graceful and the fantastic are united with a deep understanding of the human heart. Today one sees, at the beginning of the announcement of every new ballet, two or three authors' names, among which that of the choreographer features only for the *mise en scène* or, as the newspapers too often report, for the translation of the theme into pirouettes and entrechats!!! Is it due to this or that professional writer's remarkable understanding of dance steps, or to a total lack of invention on the part of the *maîtres de ballet*? Is it in order to speed up the creation of the work, or as an insurance against failure, that so many other authors must be associated with the work whilst the practical man is forced to forego any recognition for its conception? The fact is that a work for which the responsibility has been shared must necessarily deprive those involved of any notion of self-esteem and becomes something which robs the artist of his due glory. Apart from this, the librettos of the very limited repertory of ballets at the Opéra are not distinguished by the elegance of their style; on the contrary, they contain comments and sentences of dialogue impossible to express in pantomime, unless one were to use the deaf and dumb alphabet. One can search in vain in them for an incident which has not been found hundreds of times before in all the known ballets, and

[6] Among the five French choreographers listed here, Charles-Louis Didelot (1767–1837) is of particular importance since he and Bournonville kept a regular correspondence for many years. Didelot had, furthermore, been a close friend of Bournonville's father, Antoine, and in many ways stood as the young Bournonville's main choreographic ideal.

which has not been borrowed from the poems of comic operas and from boulevard entertainments.

How many times has *la Sylphide* not been traduced? And *la Diablerie*? Here is a genre which, I think, has developed to an astonishing degree, and I believe I have guessed the reason for this.

As soon as a female dancer has created a *sensation* at la *Scala* or at *San Carlo* (since in Italy there is no intermediate expression between a sensation and a *fiasco*), they summon her to Paris, and the ballet makers are given the task of concocting a showcase for her, decorated with *arabesques*, that is, a work composed especially for her. A way has to be found of including all the ballerina's most effective accomplishments, as well as her obligatory costume. If neither the former nor the latter are suited to the rôles of princess, shepherdess or divinity, they will opt for the *infernal* genre, since a doomed soul, a demon or a goddaughter of Satan can allow herself all manner of risqué activity, and the authors, indulging themselves in hallucinations, are not at all bothered by the troublesome demands of common sense.

It is not possible to judge the abilities of the present choreographers at l'Académie impériale without knowing whether or not they have submitted themselves willingly to the ungrateful task of composing their ballets according to others' ideas. In my soul and conscience I believe them to be the victims of an unfair lack of trust, and I would bet a thousand to one that none of them has dared to propose anything as delightful as *Orfa* or *les Elfes* as a subject for a ballet.[7]

[7] The two Paris Opéra ballets by Joseph Mazilier which Bournonville assesses here, with a clear touch of irony, are: (1) Mazilier's two-act pantomimic ballet on Nordic mythology *Orfa* (set to a score by Adolphe Adam, première 29 December 1852); (2) his three-act pantomimic ballet *Les Elfes* (première 11 August 1856, to a score by Nicolo Gabrielli). Although Bournonville assessed *Orfa* in very negative terms, he actually drew some important inspiration from this work for his own three Nordic-mythological ballets, in particular *The Lay of Thrym* (première at Copenhagen's Royal Theatre on 21 February 1868).

We have reached the point where we require a *ballet d'action* to be nothing but a shimmering diorama, a colourful masquerade, fireworks, a crowd of pretty *figurantes*, and finally, a *prima ballerina di cartello* capable of enduring the exertions of four good French danseuses; in fact, with twenty dance entrances, each more difficult than the last, she has certainly earned her pay, and one is led to believe that one has witnessed a choreographic creation.

In order not to end this letter like the previous ones, with an outburst of bitterness, allow me to return for a moment to the time when one left a ballet performance with the same sensations that one feels after having seen a good play, perfectly performed, at the Comédie Française.

Could one today imagine that mimes like *Goyon*, *Beaupré*, and *Ferdinand* performed the comic rôles with such great wit?[8] that *Milon* and *Albert* knew not only how to express the passions, but that they were even able, by their noble demeanour, to speak the language of reason? What love, playfulness and conviction there was in *la Somnambule*, by Mme *Montessu*![9] What sweet

[8] The three French mime artists mentioned here are Goyon (?–1815), Charles Beaupré (1758–1842), and Ferdinand (stage name for Jean La Brunière de Médicis, 1791–1837).

[9] The French ballerina Pauline Montessu (b. Paul, 1805–1877) created a stir when performing the predominantly mimic rôle of Thérèse in Jean Aumer's three-act ballet *La Somnambule, ou l'Arrivée d'un nouveau seigneur* at its Paris Opéra première on 19 September 1827 to a score composed and arranged by Ferdinand Hérold. She was also assessed by Bournonville in 1824–1825 with these words: "Slight physique fitting to the genre she dances. Graceful legs, *cou-de-pied* of steel, perfect pointes, powerful and yet light at the same time, extraordinary spirit of strength and brilliance, ardour, even gentleness in the wildness of her dance, which is often falsely called grace, arms expressive, she turns little and acts well with her kind of mimic." (*See* Knud Arne Jürgensen, *The Bournonville Tradition, The First Fifty Years 1829–1879*, vol. 1, p. 13, London, Dance Books, 1997.)

melancholy in the features of Mlle *Noblet*![10] But above them all hovered the spirit, even the *genius*, of Mlle *Bigottini*.[11] As beautiful as Mlle *Mars*, she had in her glance and in her movements the same *sweetness* which made the voice of that great actress so irresistible.

Being by turns pathetic, sensitive, noble and effervescent, she knew how to achieve a total metamorphosis and was capable, in any of her rôles, of presenting a new side of her immense talent to the astonished spectator. *Danseuse par excellence*, never aiming at astonishing effects, she sacrificed, with exquisite tact, her own *virtuosity* to the character of the rôle. Thus, when with the heart moved, the eyes still wet with tears, one left the performance, one's thoughts were neither of the dancer nor of the author, it was *Nina*, it was *Clary*, whom one had seen;[12] one had *witnessed* a series of events; art had triumphed.

AUGUST BOURNONVILLE

---

[10] Lise Noblet (1805–1877) was a leading ballerina at the Paris Opéra during the pre-Romantic and early Romantic ballet, creating, among many leading parts, the rôle of Effie in Filippo Taglioni's epoch-making *La Sylphide* (1832).

[11] Emilie Bigottini (1784–1858), perhaps the leading pre-Romantic ballerina in Paris, is often credited for having been among the first ballerinas who, in the first two decades of the nineteenth century, employed dancing on pointes in a truly artistic manner.

[12] Bigottini's two title-rôles referred to here by Bournonville are (1) Louis Milon's two-act pantomimic ballet *Nina, ou La Folle par amour* (première 23 November 1813, to a score by Louis-Luc Persuis), and (2) Milon's three-act pantomimic ballet *Clari, ou La Promesse de mariage* (première 19 June 1820 to a score by Rodolphe Kreutzer).

THE SEVENTH LETTER

(continued)

In any kind of theatrical performance, it is important to lead the spectator into a sphere of illusion not too far removed from reality. It is prose drama and grand opera which occupy the extremes of this ideal circle, with vaudeville, comic opera, verse drama, and ballet d'action occupying the centre grounds, and the mind allows itself to be transported there, provided a sense of logical action is present, and if there are no offensive naïvities of dubious taste involved.

Ballet is equally close to the plastic arts, to drama and to music, seeking its distinctive character in the beauty of form, the expression of feeling and the rhythms of melody; therefore the theory of the Dance, motivated by pantomime, can be expressed in a few words:

Everything that is *forced* ceases to be graceful. Affectation and mannerism exclude the idea of nobility.

Decency can be regarded as a conventional feeling, but an instinctive sense of *modesty* is inseparable from grace.

Dancing which does not exude intelligence becomes an act of insanity.

Nothing is as difficult and as rare as *tranquil beauty*; nothing is as easy and commonplace as *tormented ugliness*.

In Dance everything *ugly* is essentially bad.

I do not fear any objection against these simple and precise principles on the part of *male dancers*, first because there are so few of them, and second because they are not much in favour with currently predominant opinion; but I expect violent protests on the part of the young and brilliant section of the Nymphs and Bacchantes. Is it your intention, they will say to me, to force us to adapt our kind of dance to all those more or less rococo rôles that the capriciousness of any *maître de ballet* chooses to impose upon us! We will then have to return to the *menuet* or to the *sarabande*, so as to comply with the habits of the salons, and to wear villagers' clogs if the situation requires it! To please the poets and the painters, are we to be requested to renounce the audience's ovations, which boost our courage and ensure our fortune! –

I will answer them with all the sweetness of persuasion: just as in the Opéra, the *princess* would be wrong to sing in the same tone as the *mill-girl*, even though the exact imitation of nature would not allow running trills by either one of them, you will have to use your talent within the limits dictated by the nature of the scene. You will, indeed, fail to attract all the attention, but the work within which you will thus shine with only a moderate brightness will remain in the repertory. You will not be putting all your eggs in one basket, but you will be gaining the advantage of neither abusing the freshness of your talent nor the enthusiasm of the audience. They may praise you a little less, perhaps, as a dancer, as a fantastic being, but they will speak of you as a distinguished artist, as an amiable and spirited woman.

One more assault to bear and I will conclude:

This is the great question of *costumes*, a matter capable of filling an entire, lavishly illustrated book with each design more ridiculous than the last.

Since the influence of *Noverre* abolished *paniers* and *tonnelets*, we have seen the draperies of antiquity, Turkish *cafetans*, mediaeval jerkins, and the *bombais* of the Colin undergoing every change of fashion and adapting to all the requirements of the Dance. A profusion of gold and spangles, floating feathers, snow-like coiffures, puffed-out sleeves and enormous *berrets* have, in turn, defied both history and common sense, to the despair of the authors. Only the costumes of the extras could give any satisfaction to the designer or to those who search for some hint of authentic local character in the ballet ensemble.

I fear that I am repeating myself in pointing out that the Dance cannot escape the laws of dramatic action without degenerating into mere *gymnastics*.

Let a band of minstrels or bohemians join a festival; let fantastic figures appear in a dream and you may allow them to wear whatever their fancy dictates; but for a grand lady arriving with her cavalier to preside over a ceremonial ball to remove her silk robe, and reappear in a transparent tunic reaching to just above her knee, with rose-coloured legs and feet, in order to dance one of those famous *pas de deux* with a stranger dressed as a rope dancer, seems to me to be overstepping the limits of the ridiculous.

Far be it from me to undervalue the stressful and dangerous occupation of *acrobats* and *equestrian gymnasts*, but it is always with a feeling of sadness that I watch their wonders of strength and boldness. The dangers they must face, their forced jollity and their garments cut according to the needs of the *trampoline* and of the *unbridled horses*, deprive one of any artistic thoughts; but when one looks at the costumes of today's ballets, and particularly at those of the *pas de deux*, one is unpleasantly struck by their similarity to the not very aristocratic fraternity mentioned above.

I once found myself laughing at a print representing the interior of the *Circus*, but, three steps away, I saw one of a backstage scene at the Opéra, and I was seized with indignation by the caricature which had been made of the cradle of my apprenticeship! – Well! I have once again seen that cradle, and that print had in no way exaggerated the immodest dress of the female dancers. Sitting in the stalls, I was astounded at the sight of Diana's Nymphs making their entrance – with their *heels turned out* towards the audience! – Was this a coquettish affectation or simply the innocent behaviour of the daughters of the Southern sea?

If Dance academies or classes of perfection were capable of nurturing and spreading principles of good taste and of fighting that mistakenly light-hearted attitude which aims at effects alien to art, I would have started with them in my search for the source of good as well as that of evil, and I would have blamed the teachers both for the progress of the dance and for its moral decay; but that is not the case. In Paris we have nothing but *imitative academies.* The models come from abroad. One has only to copy them faithfully, in sufficient numbers, in order to people our second-rate theatres and those in the provinces; the second or even third-rate examples are the models for the *quadrilles* of the corps de ballet.[1]

The pupils who read and listen to nothing but false arguments concerning their place in the theatre and in society, laugh at their teachers' protests, and ask for nothing but to learn their *craft.* Thus, these *girls* – since there are almost no *male* pupils left – submit themselves with heroic perseverance to tortures which, just like the *tournehanche* abolished by Noverre,[2] are as useless as they are ridiculous, and strive, thanks to a marked degree of *carelessness* regarding both dress and behaviour, to overcome the natural bashfulness which could hinder their success in the career which awaits them.

You can see, Sir, that in that respect there is nothing to hope

---

[1] The hierarchical structure of the Paris Opéra Ballet was (and is still) divided into several subcategories of dancers of which the *quadrille* is among the lowest.

[2] The *tournehanche* is a wooden instrument designed to improve the turn-out of the ballerina's legs by forcing her to do her daily footwork exercises at the *barre* within the narrow space of two parallel pieces of wood.

for regarding the reforms of which I dream and which all the friends of the stage desire: doubtless, I do not feel strong enough to carry out all alone an unequal fight against the mistakes sanctified by routine and by the shared approval of a whole faction; but the most rigorous rules, the co-operation of the greatest dance celebrity, the best will of a director, and even the power of a minister, would not be enough without the participation of an *enlightened and benevolent audience*.

I will call upon all those men of intelligence whom I mentioned in my second letter, and I will make an appeal to all healthy spirits devoid of prejudice, to all honest hearts, and above all to men of letters, those fearless guides in the eternal struggle which man's spirit and the sane doctrines of art wage against obscurantism and corruption. It has been said that the theatre shapes the taste of the people, but I am not afraid to state the paradox that, if the theatre has any hope of maintaining its dignity, it will be thanks to the influence of its true audience.

The Parisian public is considered to be Europe's most appreciative and truly indulgent audience – provided however that the artist is allowed to approach it.

I will not deal with the doors double-locked by intrigue and the other special forms of protection, but rather with those groups of sycophants and claques which prevent serious opinion from being expressed, and harm the actors with cheers as dangerous to them as the intoxication of a blasé and depraved taste. How are we to extirpate this leprosy from Paris's theatres? What kind of demonstration will it take to wipe it out? When will we finally get rid of this false coinage?

It is true: the theatre auditoriums would experience a moment of unusual calm, and would resound less often to storms of applause; but a spontaneous gesture of approval would make a very different impression on the artist, and being no longer separated from the audience by intermediaries, mutual esteem and good will could be established between the stage and the public.

This mutual esteem is the first tenet of a *theatrical education*. It is first of all necessary to establish that the art used as a means of recreation for a strong and spirited nation must be both an honest form of pleasure and an honourable profession.

It is surely not rich people who devote themselves to an arduous artistic career, much less to the hazards of the theatre, but education, and above all a carefully considered education, cannot but help develop natural ability in any genre; therefore parents who are able to instil religious principles and good behaviour into their children, need not be afraid either of taking them to the theatre or placing them there professionally, if they have a strong sense of vocation. I would say to the public in the auditorium: praise great talents, but do not forget to encourage the diligent ones; strike with disapproval at poor behaviour, but do not pay attention to gossip; try to ignore small backstage troubles and treat with disdain those bad plays which feed the appetite for scandal by revealing so-called secrets, thereby defaming honourable citizens and filling their hearts with the bitterness of injustice, and sometimes making them indifferent to the opinion of their fellow men.

I would tell the *general public*: cross out in the dictionary the word *bohème* when it refers to artists. Believe in virtue and if you find it among people of the theatre, their social position ought not to prevent you from behaving virtuously in their presence. As for the second-rank artist, who has no hope of attracting the audience's attention, compensate him with your personal esteem, and if, by chance, you should discover in him some human weakness, do not ascribe this to his profession.

These remarks, which concern theatrical life in general, may lead us too far away; I resign myself to returning to my speciality and I address myself to the young artists and the pupils who, for the most part, have chosen the hard and often thankless career of the dance for no other reason than the lack of the time and the means with which to develop those qualities needed for other branches of the theatre.

As regards their life in the *theatre*, I will tell them:

Do not forget that what you are doing is an *art*, do not be afraid of facing the difficulties which will lead you to *true beauty*; disdain any charlatanism and reject anything that seems indecent to you. Beware of the weakness of self-esteem and pay no heed to excessive praise. Try to please rather than to astonish: *frenzy* diminishes, *pleasure* grows. Always prefer a moderate income with a secure position, and one that is socially respected, to the uncertain life of the traveller, and do not allow yourself to be dazzled by the vaunted prestige of fabulous salaries.

For everyday life, I will speak to them as a father: regard yourself as belonging to the big family of industrious people; do not look for future happiness in riches and idleness, but work to achieve an honest prosperity and an old age free from regrets. Do not try to live above your means; shine on stage, but be retiring in your private life; your habits and your education entitle you to be part of the intelligent middle class, but consider *the good and the great* only as *examples* to be studied from a distance, without joining in their games. Despite their assurances of their disinterested protection – they can't help it – you will always be a mere instrument in their eyes. Defend with all your eloquence the rights of your art against its detractors; give proof of its dignity on stage by your talent; in society, by your behaviour; and if one day, after having diligently achieved your goal, fortune allows you to enjoy the fruits of your labours, beware of discrediting the profession which earned you a living.

I would have much more to say to the teachers and to the choreographers, but they are my colleagues, my companions who I can address in person; moreover, if they have read my letters carefully and above all with the good will that should bring us closer together, they will have understood me perfectly.

Allow me, in my next [and last] letter, to imagine myself the head of the Opéra's administration, presenting myself with a project for the reorganisation of the ballet.

AUGUST BOURNONVILLE

THE EIGHTH LETTER

(continued and concluded)

If the glorious, intelligent, virtuous nation of France were to put the care of an artistic institution in my hands, not only with the responsibility for its finances, but also for its progress, I would not regard myself as *le maître* of Parnassus, but as the humble and faithful servant of the Muses and the Graces. Taken literally, these responsibilities would make it my duty to take a whip to the second-hand merchants obstructing the approaches to the temple and to chase them away, and to borrow the strength of *Hercules* to evacuate the *Augean stables* . . . But, being obliged to tread a positive path, and aiming only at the dignity of the stage and at the honour of the theatrical profession, I would simply begin:

"*To remove* from the boundary of l'Académie impériale de musique the *bacchic festivities of the carnival.* These balls violate the sanctuary of lyric arts, intermingling, in the name of the Opéra, extravagance and debauchery.

"*To prohibit* any unauthorised person access to the wings, to the foyer, or to the dressing rooms. – The intimate acquaintances made by means of such access harm the work of the theatre and the reputation of the artists.

"*To ban* complimentary tickets, other than reduced-price admittance for the authors, and personal passes for the artists. – If all the tickets were for sale at the box office, the cabal could only be *bought off* by paying through the nose, and it would be difficult to arrange for a *paid claque* to take over the middle of the auditorium.

"*To forbid*, the penalty being a large fine, the artists to discard the character of their rôles in order to take curtain calls, or to make provocative gestures towards the audience in response to their applause. If prolonged acclamations did not bring the object of their real or false enthusiasm back to the front of the stage, if the flowers and wreaths were respectfully gathered up by a stage hand, then the performance would be less frequently interrupted by ovations, some of them very much out of place, and the acclaimed artists would not be constantly tempted to disregard the limits of art and of common sense in order to achieve triumphs which, once they start waning, leave a sense of emptiness and despair in the soul . . . "

As regards internal discipline, I would adhere rigidly to the politeness and to the tactful conventions of decent society; I would allow neither bad habits nor the informalities of bad taste, and I would punish severely any man – even if he were the leading singer – who allowed himself to mouth indecencies in the presence of women or children.

Far be it from me to inquire into private habits or behaviour; I would pretend to ignore any kind of relationship outside the theatre; but I would make it a point of honour, for the institution's sake, that the scandal which has been far too much associated with this or that artistic rank, should, in the interest of art and humanity, be confined to the shadows of the past, and not displayed and justified in the eyes of the world.

Nevertheless, not being able to forego the desire of seeing talents enhanced by education and good behaviour, I would like to establish, alongside specialised teaching, a *high school* directed by experienced people whose religious and moral piety might coincide with the idea of the lofty aims of theatrical art. I would invite artistic celebrities, as well as famous literary figures, to join me in this praiseworthy task of giving classes suitable for young people in order to instil in them the firm belief that all the arts – even that of the dance – are linked to each other in a single chain, which must lead to the ennoblement and the glory of nations.

As money is at the nerve centre of any enterprise, in this world, I would not refuse to countenance reforms concerning economics, and I would begin with the *takings*.

I would not be afraid of seeing a reduction in numbers, since I would have struck a blow at the taste of the *bored faction*, who, no doubt, would protest loudly against any restriction placed on their abusive behaviour, against the reforming of the genres, and against the moderate progress of the *chariot* which they believed to be proceeding at full speed, but which had been tumbling rapidly down a fatal slope. This faction will refer mockingly to the temple of good manners, to virtuous entrechats, to pirouettes à la vestale – they will turn their backs on the Théâtre de l'Opéra, and will go elsewhere in search of pleasures more suited to their inclinations, and we will wish them good riddance; but the huge majority of those who love good music, dramatic singing and ballet's attractive and varied tableaux will be delighted to see once again a spectacle freed from corrupting influences; and even those who, previously, were repulsed by the extravagances which had usurped the domain of the arts, will now return once more to refresh and fortify their spirits.

As for the rest, the whole nation will know *why and to what end* it maintains, with its own means, such a lavishly subsidised institution.

With regard to the *budget for expenditure*, I could surely accept the financial sacrifices that the splendour of a spectacle worthy of the capital of a great empire would entail, but I would not overburden with luxury works which should earn their success by real merit, and if, in an opera as well as in a ballet, I should notice that the profusion of tableaux, instead of underpinning the action, only served to conceal the lack of interest, I would do without this kind of masterpiece and would make better use of the amounts of money such opulent magnificence demands.

I would never sacrifice the interests of a staff of four hundred people to the exorbitant demands of some *premiers sujets di cartello*. The Paris Opéra, being an *academy* (and not a limited partnership subject to bankruptcies and completely alien to artistic considerations, as well as to alterations suggested by human vanities), must pay its artists honourably, but never be subject to their capricious will. – Is it still an honour to be employed there? Is it still regarded as the baptismal font of European fame, or do those who work there look for nothing but the advantages offered by the fair of Senigaglia?[1] – Anyhow, I would not countenance extortion, even if it were demanded by some pressing situation concerning the salary of France's marshal. Taking the salary paid to the *premiers sujets* as a yardstick, according to the 1830 rate – I would add *one third* in consideration of the high cost of living, and I would go up to a maximum of 40,000 francs *per annum*, to avoid dropping to a *minimum* below the tolerable.

I will be told that I would then have to forego engaging Europe's great celebrities, monopolised as they would be by the markets of *London* and *Saint Petersburg*, and that the Paris Opéra would thus find itself in the second or third rank; but I would

---

[1] The annual fair in the town of Senigaglia, in the Marche region of central Italy, was the most important and famous trade fair during the Papal dominion. Its name was used as a term to indicate a major place where second-hand goods were for sale.

reply that *Paris* must claim the right to *create* theatrical reputations and not just to *house* them, even when, as often happens in their nomadic life, they have lost the freshness of their skills.

With artists formed under a progressive régime, the Opéra would have the advantage of making its repertory follow the path of a *national originality*, instead of stagnating in the rut of routine, as a mere echo of foreign scenes.

Finally, had the system followed during the last twenty years been able to make its different branches prosper, the Opéra would today exert a supremacy which it cannot claim, in spite of the enormous sums of money allocated to its budget.

I come now to the most delicate point, or rather to the open wound of the Opéra's administration, as well as that of the majority of the theatres which still look upon this academy as the example to follow. – It is the *salaries* of the lower ranks, in particular of the members of the corps de ballet.

The lavishness of the performance requires dancing masses and a great crowd of people or of fantastic beings, according to the nature of the subject, and the eye is pleasantly surprised at seeing them move towards the footlights with such gay abandon! One takes pleasure in repeating this delicious refrain from a romance in *la Lampe merveilleuse*:

"Venez, charmantes bayadères!
Venez, enfants de la gaité,
Commencez vos danses légères,
Image de la volupté." [2]

And one seems to forget that the *bayadères*, priestesses devoted to

[2] "Come, charming bayadères!/Come, children of merriment/Commence your light-hearted dances/The image of voluptuousness." This quotation is from Nicolo Isouard's three-act fairy-opera *Aladin, ou La Lampe merveilleuse*, premièred at the Paris Opéra on 6 February 1822.

the same mysteries which stigmatised paganism at the time of the apostles – are indeed the *children of sorrow*: the ones that oblige you to laugh and to dance with a broken heart! Well! Look at that phalanx of sylphs maintaining a carefree smile whilst holding their dying sister in their arms! This light-hearted group consists of two categories of female dancers: the first who hope to achieve talent, and the second who forever will be frustrated by it. The first group consists of the youngest and usually the prettiest. They have been reared in poverty but with a lot of ambition. The only reward for their hard work is, in most cases, the meagre nourishment provided by parents impatient to see them *earn their living*! They must pay their teacher and *behave themselves*, and the administration employs them *gratis* or for an insignificant fee. The others, older and less gifted by nature, have seen all their efforts frustrated by the twin obstacles of a poor physique and bad luck; they do their duty, cast an indifferent glance at the brilliantly gifted, and try to banish from their thoughts the prospect of retirement, often without any hope of a pension; happy to be able to aspire to a job as an usherette! – They receive an annual salary ranging from one-thousand to four hundred francs! And their dances are meant to portray an image of sensuous enjoyment. – Cruel irony!

Laugh, you lovers of good jokes, when, in some frivolous play, they talk about the little female dancers of the Opéra, cast a stone, you severe moralists, at these poor girls who entered the theatre at the most tender age, delighted to be dressed up as *Séraphins* at six in the evening, to feature in the clouds of an apotheosis at midnight . . . and who, today, see their sky darken, their illusions vanish, their paradise lost!

Still in my imaginary position of theatre director, I would ask an honest woman citizen of Paris to estimate the cost of board and lodging and suitable clothing for a young person devoting herself to a hard-working career, and I would adjust, according to this information, the salary of the *dernière figurante*, always taking into consideration their relative progress and the need to encourage them, and bearing in mind the dignity of the individual and the interests of the institution. I would make the theatre pay for the pupils' classes and would ensure that they were not burdened with additional expenses.

If my budget did not allow me to pay my corps de ballet decently, I would decide to reduce it by a quadrille or two, but I could not aspire to radical reform without giving the lower ranks a completely different status to that which they have today; [perhaps I will be accused of showing socialist tendencies, but] I would consider that I was acting in the interest and for the honour of decent society.

I have expressed what my conscience as a man and as an artist commands to me [to profess], in front of all true friends of the theatre, and I end with a plea, made at *the choice of an opportune moment*, for the cause of the fine arts, in a country constantly preoccupied with major issues, where the great events in life pay scant attention to the arts, whose only purpose seems to be to provide some charm to moments of leisure in everyday life.

During my last stay in Paris, I felt the influence of a will which is not only guided by triumphal victories that speak to posterity through superb monuments, but which also rejoices in embellishing the public streets with *flowering shrubs and shady trees* and watches over the salvation of the poorest citizens.

An inner voice has urged me to write, by saying to me: perhaps one good word may be enough to help bring some order in this chaos, to champion human rights, to restore profaned altars, and to return an art, sprung from [poetic] harmony, to a situation worthy of its noble origin.

AUGUST BOURNONVILLE